Shattered Lives is a beautifully rendered and valuable addition to the growing literature on European-American internment. Russell Estlack provides excellent summaries of government policies and actions and has chosen his individual stories carefully and with compassion. This is the best treatment of the subject that I know of for a general audience.

—Stephen "Steve" Fox, PhD, author of
Homeland Security and *Fear Itself*

—— RUSSELL W. ESTLACK ——

SHATTERED
LIVES
SHATTERED
DREAMS

THE DISRUPTED LIVES OF FAMILIES IN
AMERICA'S INTERNMENT CAMPS

BONNEVILLE BOOKS
SPRINGVILLE, UTAH

ISBN 13: 978-1-59955-796-0

Published by Bonneville Books, an imprint of Cedar Fort, Inc.
2373 W. 700 S., Springville, UT 84663
Distributed by Cedar Fort, Inc., www.cedarfort.com

LIBRARY OF CONGRESS CATALOGING-IN-PUBLICATION DATA

Estlack, Russell W., author.
  Shattered lives, shattered dreams : the disrupted lives of families in america's internment camps / Russell W. Estlack.
    pages cm
  Includes bibliographical references.
  ISBN 978-1-59955-796-0
  1. Concentration camps--United States. 2. World War, 1939-1945--Concentration camps--United States. 3. Prisoners of war--United States--History--20th century. I. Title.

  D805.U5E85 2011
  940.53'1773--dc22

                              2011002690

Cover design by Danie Romrell
Cover design © 2011 by Lyle Mortimer
Typeset by Megan Welton

Printed in the United States of America

10 9 8 7 6 5 4 3 2 1

Printed on acid-free paper

ACKNOWLEDGMENTS

I would like to express my appreciation to all of the people who made this book possible. Special thanks to Art Jacobs and *The Freedom of Information Times*; Karen Ebel; Heidi Donald; Doris Nye; and Eberhard Fuhr, along with the members of the German American Internee Coalition who provided much of the research material for this book. I am also grateful to all of the families who allowed me to share their stories in the hope that they will never be forgotten. And thanks as well to my editor, Lana Jordan, for her professional work and attention to detail.

Those who cannot remember the past are doomed to repeat it.

—George Santayana

We learn from history that we learn nothing from history.

—George Bernard Shaw

What experience and history teach is this—that people and governments never have learned anything from history, or acted on principles deduced from it.

—Georg Wilhelm Friedrich Hegel

CONTENTS

FAITH OVER FEAR WHEN CALLED AN ENEMY

In his work *Shattered Lives, Shattered Dreams*, Russell Estlack has produced a fresh look at the incarceration of eleven thousand German Americans out of the sixty thousand who were arrested shortly after the bombing of Pearl Harbor. This is a necessary study of an injustice that is largely unknown in America, and if known, dismissed as unimportant, exaggerated, or not having transpired at all. It is a story that needs to be told and retold again and again. Mr. Estlack tells the story with documented information, penetration, empathy, and power. It needs to have the widest circulation and discussion within and outside of the academy, the legislative halls, service clubs, and church meeting rooms. There is a longing in these pages, a yearning, and a thirst for both appropriate mercy and fair justice. Read the book. Unforgettable.

True stories have to be told. Some of these stories have been told. All of these stories need to be told. Karen Ebel, a non-practicing lawyer and one of the leaders in the cause of these German Americans, describes how her father, Max, fled Germany to avoid involvement with the Third Reich. Yet, in America he was subjected to conditions described as hell. When they were interned, the assumption was that they had done something wrong. In the case of Mr. Ebel, Art Jacobs, Eberhard Fuhr, and thousands of others, it was an atmosphere of racism, community hysteria, gossip, shoddy legal protections, and denial of rights that landed these loyal Americans in jail. These individuals were essentially an immigrant group of people, coming to America, a land of promise and hope. In most instances, they were hard working and fixed on making a living and surviving. They left an uncertain Germany and Europe, and in coming to this land were met with a surprising loss of rights, dignity, property, and reputation.

Art Jacobs said that life would never be the same again and that household furnishings and reputations were gone as well. Eberhard Fuhr, an athlete, was denied the freedoms of those late teenage years when two federal agents dragged him out of a high school in Cincinnati, Ohio. He was not released until five years later. He met his wife while imprisoned at Crystal City. Amazingly, at the age of eighty-three, instead of being bitter, he continues to tell his story with objectivity, knowledge, and insight that inspires all who hear it.

The amazing fact in this unjust internment is that no overt act of sabotage was ever committed by any of these internees, and sixty-five years after the conclusion of World War II, it is time enough to recognize this salient truth. There were naturalized citizens and American citizens caught up in the net of incarceration. These experiences became nightmares for these people, the majority of whom were struggling as working citizens in a new land. The memories of injustice even drove some of them to return to wartime Germany, where additional hardship, injustice, and fear of constant death followed their very steps until many of them eventually came back to the United States. The voyage of the MS *Gripsholm* to wartime Germany to repatriate some of these German internees is a horror story in itself.

Of course, there was considerable anti-German sentiment in those years. The media did its utmost to inflame public opinion against all things German and under-reported crimes and atrocities committed by the allies. There was an open season on all ethnic German Americans, in spite of the fact that German ancestry was part of most Americans' heritage. The propaganda and the wrongs of the Hitler regime made anti-German sentiment popular.

The Lutheran Church could have protested against the internment, but in too many instances, they lacked the awareness of the U.S. Constitution, American history, and their responsibilities as good citizens and good parishioners to speak up. While I love and respect our dear Lutheran Christian Church, in a number of cases, even the pastors were reluctant to speak for the defense of the German Americans lest they also be incriminated.

From 1939 to 1947, my three brothers and I attended the Immanuel Lutheran School in Bristol, Connecticut. To be sure, we had racist, anti-German statements coming at us and even had childhood altercations over this issue. Though we considered ourselves Americans with both of our parents born in America, our grandparents were born as ethnic Germans in Poland. The changing borders in that part of the world for much of the twentieth century compelled me to travel to Poland, Russia, and Europe a half dozen times to study the issues of families on both sides of conflicts, deportations, and various oppressions. The memory of discrimination in my youth hounded me, and for the past forty years I have committed myself to speaking, marching, writing, and teaching on issues of discrimination, injustice, and racism, not only in the U.S., but also throughout this broken world.

It must be emphasized that in my own congregation in Bristol, Connecticut, out of about a thousand souls, two hundred served in the armed forces, and four made the supreme sacrifice. We were citizens of this blessed land, and we were encouraged to support all the defense drives and stamp collections. But deep down, in our hearts, we prayed that our families, even those on the "enemy" side, would somehow be protected in this war where people were killing each other. As Abraham Lincoln stated in his Second Memorial Address, "The purpose of this nation is to bind up the wounds on both sides, to take care of the widows and those who lost their homes." This memorable address should serve as a model for how victors should treat the vanquished.

I have never forgotten that inner conflict. It was projected into our own American Civil War and other subsequent wars where families were divided. I am certain that it is present with people of the Muslim faith. As a citizen of this blessed land, one is obligated to serve, protect, and assist the country. Yet, biblical laws of praying for the enemy were epitomized by the great English Christian scholar C. S. Lewis who got down on his knees to pray that the minds and spirits of even Hitler and Stalin, notorious genocidal murderers, would be transformed and that they would change their orientation.

Works by Alfred de Zayas, Brigitte Neary, Evelyne Tannehill, Julius Loisch, and others have demonstrated that atrocities are committed by both sides, and that fear, fanaticism, and frenzy have to be moved toward reconciliation. These same principles apply in today's global struggle. The nuclear weapons of various nations make it mandatory that some type of modus operandi be achieved. In a drone, digital age where terrorists can commit mass murder with the push of a button, we are all endangered. I pray that somehow a merciful God will hold the Sword of Damocles back, and that we will find a way to move toward reconciliation instead of demonization. In this sense too, Mr. Estlack's book is cogent and timely for our current convoluted climate of terror.

Mr. Estlack has done a commendable job. He brought the story up close to present-day issues of terrorism, U.S. constitutional rights, the twentieth century history of controversy, and let us say it—perhaps a residual bias against things German for over three generations. As we deal with the fanaticism, terrorism, and false religion of our day, this book is highly recommended as a primary resource of reflection.

Shattered Lives, Shattered Dreams is an unforgettable book about an enduring American story. It deserves the widest circulation throughout the United States and abroad.

—Dr. Albert E. Jabs
Martin Luther King Speaker
Valparaiso University

PREFACE

If the first casualty of war is truth, then questionable government actions, cover-ups, and revisionist accounts of history must be the ultimate casualties of peace. Governments will go to any lengths to hide the truth from their citizens. Most Americans are familiar with the relocation and detainment of Japanese Americans during World War II. Thanks to the efforts of the United States Government, the facts surrounding the internment and repatriation of German aliens during two world wars have until recently been hidden from the American people. The evidence is overwhelming, but government leaders, historians, and academics at some of the most prestigious colleges and universities in America refuse to acknowledge these events.

The internment of German aliens had its genesis in the Alien Enemies Act of 1798 and the wartime policies of Woodrow Wilson. Revered by academics and historians for his progressive agenda, they seldom if ever mention that Wilson was an avowed racist who ordered the segregation of the military and all civil service offices and brought Jim Crow to Washington. Wilson's disregard for the rights of African-Americans and his refusal to act against racial violence is exceeded by his administration's repression of dissent and curtailment of civil liberties during the war years.

President Franklin Delano Roosevelt inherited Wilson's legacy and continued to abuse the civil liberties of the American people and violate the precepts of the U.S. Constitution in the name of national security. Roosevelt built on the laws passed by Congress and signed into law by President Wilson to issue Presidential orders authorizing the arrest, internment, and repatriation of German, Italian, and Japanese nationals, along with American citizens he considered a dangerous threat to national security. With the cooperation and blessing of certain South American governments, he ordered the kidnapping and detainment of thousands of German and Japanese nationals from Latin America.

The mind-set of the American people in the early years of the twentieth century was far different than it is today. The First World War was raging in Europe, and given the acts of sabotage by enemy agents on American soil, persons with foreign names, especially Germans, were under suspicion. When America entered the war, all Germans were suspect and became the recipients of unreasonable ethnic and racial violence, and in some cases, imprisonment for the duration of the war.

Ethnic hatred once again reared its ugly head with the attack on Pearl Harbor and Hitler's invasion of Europe. Songs, movies, and news articles promoted Americanism like a sacred mantra, and the Axis empires of Germany, Italy, and Japan were considered evil incarnate. Racial and language differences between individuals living in America took on a new and sinister meaning. Hysteria and fear dictated that arrest, relocation, internment, and repatriation of enemy aliens were the only way to safeguard the country.

The events that drove the internments created a perceived need for laws to prevent further acts of sabotage and terrorism and to protect the American people from the perpetrators of those acts. Like the Alien Enemies Act of 1798, many of those laws have never been rescinded. They have formed the foundation for new laws that further restrict our freedoms and, in many cases, violate one or more amendments of the Constitution.

With the attack on the World Trade Center and the Pentagon on September 11, 2001, ethnic animosity has now been transferred to Muslims and Arabs. Some of the laws passed by Congress in the angry and emotional aftermath of 9/11 and the actions taken by the government to enforce those laws are in many ways similar to the laws and actions of previous administrations. In the rush to protect its citizens, the principles that America was built on and the Constitution that guarantees the freedoms so many Americans fought and died for appear to have been ignored or forgotten.

Can it happen again? In the postscript to his book, *America's Invisible Gulag*, Stephen Fox wrote, "After I published *The Unknown Internment* in 1990, many people asked me whether I thought "it" could happen again. America had learned *something* from history, had it not? The answer is both yes and no. I suggested that the beast might simply appear in a different garb, and offered some broad examples: our propensity to simplify problems by categorizing people; by associating them (racial profiling of any sort); by criminalizing their thoughts and behavior. "It" happens every time we think of "us" versus "them"; every time we marginalize a people by emphasizing their "alienness" and put them beyond society's protection as though they were science fiction extraterrestrials."[1]

For more than one hundred years, ethnic minorities in America have been the target of hatred and violence. The Reverend Martin Niemöller was imprisoned in two of Hitler's death camps from 1941 to 1945. His famous poem "First They Came for the Communist" carries a powerful message to future generations:

> First they came for the communist, and I did not speak out
> because I was not a communist.
> Then they came for the socialist, and I did not speak out
> because I was not a socialist.
> Then they came for the trade unionist, and I did not speak out
> because I was not a trade unionist.
> Then they came for the Jews, and I did not speak out
> because I was not a Jew.
> Then they came for me—
> and there was no one left to speak for me.

NOTES

1. Stephen Fox, *America's Invisible Gulag: A Biography of German American Internment & Exclusion in World War II* (New York: Peter Lang, 2000).

ONE

HISTORIC REALITY

Most Americans are familiar with the shameful injustices per-petrated against Japanese Americans during the dark days of World War II. The forced relocation and internment of Japanese Americans living on the west coast of the United States has been well documented, and they have received compensation and an apology from the U.S. government.

Less known is the fact that from 1941 to 1948, more than ten thousand German Americans were arrested and interned in sixty camps across the United States and Hawaii. It didn't matter how long they'd lived in the United States or whether they were natu-ralized American citizens. As long as they retained their social and cultural traits and continued to speak their own language or spoke English with a German accent, the government considered them a threat to the security of the United States.

When Americans are asked about it, they almost always respond, "I didn't know that" or "I've never heard that before." Until recently, the government has done its best to keep the American public in the dark. Government agencies, including the State Department, the Justice Department, and the FBI, masterfully covered their tracks, but under the Freedom of Information Act, they've been forced to grant access to many of the records of wartime activities. Even up to the present day, some records are still classified and not available to the general public.

There is no mention of these events in history books, and public schools, colleges, and universities teach that no Germans or Italians were ever arrested or interned. Newspaper editors write editorials that deny the truth, but their archives are rife with articles that tell the whole story. Under the circumstances, it's easy to understand why the American public has little knowledge of the terrible injustices done to the nation's German population during World War II.

There is a historical precedent for government action in this matter. During World War I, 2,048 Germans were interned at Fort Oglethorpe, Georgia, and Fort Douglas, Utah. It wasn't until a year after the Versailles Treaty was signed that the last two hundred internees were released and the camps closed. Vigilantism, harassment, vandalism, looting, and violence were driven by hate, hysteria, and mob rule. At least one German was accused of being a spy. He was tarred, feathered, and lynched by a frenzied mob at Collinsville, Illinois, for whispering a prayer in German in a dying woman's ear. The press of the day described Germans as anti-American in much the same way as the newspapers of World War II described them as Nazis.

Ethnic hatred is driven by suspicion, innuendo, rumors, and events of historic importance. From 1914 to 1918, hostile actions by the German government continued to sow the seeds of animosity. On May 7, 1915, a German U-boat, the U-20, torpedoed and sank the *Lusitania* on her maiden voyage near the coast of Ireland. Within eighteen minutes, the ship slipped beneath the waves. Of the 1,124 passengers on board, 1,119, including 114 Americans, went down with the ship.

While war raged and armies marched across the face of Europe, America chose to remain neutral. But when America shipped munitions, fuel, and explosives to British, French, and Russian troops, the German government broke its pledge to limit submarine attacks on allied shipping.

In 1916, Woodrow Wilson was elected to a second term largely because of his campaign slogan, "He kept us out of war." Despite Wilson's pledge that America would remain neutral, unrestricted submarine warfare, the Zimmerman telegram, sabotage on American soil, and the Black Tom explosion helped drag the United States into the conflict and intensified anti-German sentiment in America.

Neutrality was the official policy of the United States, but unofficially, the Wilson administration embarked on a program of military preparedness and financial and material support of England and its allies. With this change in U.S. foreign policy, the administration became increasingly concerned about criticism of its policies and pro-German propaganda. Politicians from both parties stirred the pot of ethnic hatred when they publicly questioned the loyalty of what they called "hyphenate Americans," especially Irish and German immigrants.

Twenty-six years before the attack on Pearl Harbor, President Wilson fueled the fires of anti-immigrant fervor. On December 7, 1915, in his Third Annual Message to Congress, he proclaimed, "There are citizens of the United States . . . born under other flags but welcomed by our generous naturalization laws to the full freedom and opportunity of America, who have poured the poison of disloyalty into the arteries of our national life. Such advocates of disloyalty and anarchy must be crushed out."[1]

Germany was determined to stop what they saw as shipments of contraband weapons to their enemies on the battlefield. They dispatched undercover agents to America with orders to sabotage munitions operations. As the war broke out, German agents were skulking around the United States setting off bombs and incendiary devices. Over fifty acts of sabotage were carried out on American targets, nearly thirty of them in the New York area alone.

Mysterious fires were set at military depots, manufacturing facilities, shipping lines, and railroads. On January 1, 1915, an incendiary fire in the Roebling Steel Foundry in Trenton, New Jersey, was followed in quick succession by fires and explosions in other plants and factories dealing in war contracts for the allies. The Black Tom explosion was the peak act of German sabotage on American soil during World War I, and it had a direct impact on the internment of German Americans during World War II.[2]

Black Tom Pier was a mile-long pier that jutted out into the harbor from the New Jersey waterfront to Black Tom Island near the Statue of Liberty. A major munitions depot for war materials manufactured in the northeastern United States, the pier housed a complex of warehouses, loading docks, and railroad tracks. Any time, day or night, cargo ships, lighters, barges, and tugs loaded with tons of explosives were tied up at the pier.

At 2:08 a.m. on Sunday, July 30, 1916, two million tons of war materials packed into dozens of railroad cars and barges exploded, sending massive amounts of debris into Lower Manhattan, Jersey City, Ellis Island, and New York Harbor. The explosion was the equivalent of an earthquake measuring 5.5 on the Richter scale and was felt as far away as Baltimore, Maryland.

Thousands of windows in a twenty-five mile radius were shattered, and people were thrown from their beds. Awakened by the deafening roar, thousands of New Yorkers clad in pajamas and nightgowns poured into the streets. They watched in fascinated horror as munitions exploded across the harbor and lit up the sky with a brilliant saffron hue.

The shock waves shook the Brooklyn Bridge and set off fire alarms in Lower Manhattan and Jersey City. Shrapnel pierced the arm and the torch of the Statue of Liberty, closing the arm to tourists for decades. The concrete vaulted ceiling of Ellis Island's main hall collapsed, and newly arrived immigrants were evacuated from their dormitories while hot cinders rained on them from the sky. More than five hundred people living on houseboats and barges in the harbor and ninety mental patients in a government hospital for the insane were also evacuated.

An unidentified witness in Jersey City described the holocaust as an American Verdun. "Bombs soared into the air and burst a thousand feet above the harbor into terrible yellow. Shrapnel peppered the brick walls of the warehouses, plowed the planks of the pier and rained down upon the hissing waters." After the explosions ceased and the fuel fires were extinguished, the smoke cleared to reveal a path of devastation that was several city blocks wide. Black Tom Pier and most of the island were gone.

Hundreds were injured, but amazingly only four people died as a result of the explosion: a policeman, a guard at the pier, a barge captain, and a ten-month-old infant who was thrown from his crib. Reported property damage was estimated at $20 million, and the Statue of Liberty sustained $100,000 in damages ($377 million and

$1.9 million respectively in today's dollars).

In January 1917, the British Government intercepted and deciphered a telegram from German Foreign Minister Arthur Zimmermann to von Eckhardt, the German Minister to Mexico announcing their intention to employ unrestricted submarine warfare against the allies in effort to force a peace between Germany and England. Zimmermann also offered generous financial support and agreed to give the southwestern United States to Mexico if they would join the Germans in their cause. On March 1, 1917, the American press published the news of the telegram:

> To the German Minister to Mexico
> Berlin, January 19, 1917
>
> We intend to begin on the first of February unrestricted submarine warfare. We shall endeavor in spite of this to keep the United States of America neutral. In the event of this not succeeding, we make Mexico a proposal or alliance on the following basis: make war together, make peace together, generous financial support, and an understanding on our part that Mexico is to reconquer the lost territory in New Mexico, Texas, and Arizona. The settlement of details is left to you. You will inform the President of the above most secretly as soon as war with the United States of America is certain and add the suggestion that he should, on his own initiative, invite Japan to immediate adherence and at the same time, mediate between Japan and ourselves. Please call the President's attention to the fact that the ruthless employment of our submarines now offers the prospect of compelling England in a few months to make peace.
>
> Zimmermann
> (Secretary of State)[3]

The Zimmermann telegram was the last straw. America declared war on Germany in April 1917, and Congress unanimously passed the Espionage Act of 1917 and the Sedition Act of 1918.

The Espionage Act dealt with everything from acts of espionage to protecting shipping, and for the most part wasn't controversial. However, the constitutionality of the act was called into question with the provisions that directly affected the civil liberties of

American citizens and limited or prohibited their right to free speech under the First Amendment.

> Title 1, section 3: Whoever, when the united States is at war, shall willfully make or convey false reports or false statements with intent to interfere with the operation or success of the military or naval forces of the united States or to promote the success of its enemies, and whoever when the United States is at war, shall willfully cause or attempt to cause insubordination, disloyalty, mutiny, refusal of duty, in the military or naval forces of the United States, or shall willfully obstruct the recruiting or enlistment service of the United States, to the injury of the service or of the United States, shall be punished by a fine of not more than $10,000 or imprisonment for not more than twenty years or both.

To insure that inflammatory material or information did not pass through the United State Postal Service, the Wilson Administration added Title 12 to the Espionage Act. It empowered the Postmaster General to declare any material that violated any provision of the Espionage Act that urged treason, insurrection, or forcible resistance to the authority of the United States unmailable. Use of the mail to transmit such materials was punishable by imprisonment, a fine, or both.[4]

As originally introduced, the Espionage Act gave the president power to censor the publication of any material he considered potentially useful to the enemy. This censorship provision received so much opposition from the press as well as politicians from both parties that Congress removed it from the bill. Wilson made a direct appeal to the Congress, but Congress refused to enact it.

On May 16, 1918, Congress enacted the Sedition Act, which amended the Espionage Act to add a variety of prohibitions to Title 1, Section 3. These included writing or uttering any disloyal, profane, scurrilous, or abusive language about the form of government of the United States, the military or naval forces of the United States, the flag of the United States, the uniform of the army or navy of the United States, or any language intended to bring any of the above into contempt, scorn, or disrepute. The Sedition Act further amended the Espionage Act to enhance the powers of the Postmaster General.[5]

As can be expected, the law was brought before the justices of the Supreme Court. In Schenck v. United States (1919), the court rejected the First Amendment challenge and ruled that when faced by a clear and present danger, Congress had the power to enact legislation that under ordinary circumstances might not be acceptable.

In writing the decision for the unanimous court, Justice Oliver Wendell Holmes rejected the First Amendment argument:

> The most stringent protection of free speech would not protect a man in falsely shouting fire in a theater and causing a panic. It does not even protect a man from an injunction against uttering words that may have the effect of force. The question in every case is whether the words used are used in such circumstances and are of such a nature as to create a clear and present danger that they will bring about the substantive evils that Congress has a right to prevent. It is a question of proximity and degree. When a nation is at war, many things that might be said in time of peace are such a hindrance to its effort that their utterance will not be endured so long as men fight, and that no Court could regard them as protected by any constitutional right.[6]

The war ended in 1919, and even though Wilson wanted to continue the raids, prosecution, and deportation of allegedly disloyal citizens, Congress rejected his request for a peacetime Sedition Act. The government's response to supposed sedition during and after the war concerning free speech and the loss of civil liberties brought about the creation of the American Civil Liberties Union and a broader understanding of First Amendment rights. Congress has amended the Espionage Act over the years, but it still remains a part of federal law and is the basis for the Patriot Act.

NOTES

1. Woodrow Wilson, State of the Union Address, December 7, 1915.
2. *Black Tom Explosion (1916)*, courtesy of The State of New Jersey Department of Environmental Protection, Division of Parks and Forestry, Liberty State Park Historic Collection.
3. Zimmerman Telegram, 1917; Decimal File, 1910–29, 826.20212/82A (1910–29), General Records of the Department of State, Record Group 59; National Archives.

4. Espionage Act, USC 18, PL 1, CH 37, Stat. 217, June 15, 1917.
5. Sedition Act, Vol. XL, p. 553 ff, May 16, 1918.
6. Schenck v. United States, 249 U.S. 47, March 3, 1919.

---------------------------- TWO ----------------------------

ARREST AND DETAINMENT

Prior to World War II and especially during the war, the United States government felt the need to act decisively to protect its citizens from what they considered dangerous individuals in our midst. To justify their actions, the government ignored or suspended certain civil liberties and trampled on the rights of innocent people. Government raids, ransacking of homes, selective internment, exchanges, repatriation, and exclusion were the order of the day. American citizens and legal residents of German, Italian, and Japanese ancestry were rounded up and herded into internment camps for the duration of the war and beyond.

The actions that triggered these events had their beginnings in 1936. President Franklin Delano Roosevelt was concerned with the growing militancy of Nazi Germany and the wave of espionage that had erupted across the United States the previous year. On June 26, 1939, Roosevelt signed a Presidential Directive stating:

> It is my desire that the investigation of all espionage, counter-espionage, and sabotage matters be controlled and handled by the Federal Bureau of Investigation of the Department of Justice, the Military Intelligence Division [MID] of the War Department, and the Office of Naval Intelligence [ONI] of the Navy Department. The directors of these three agencies are to function as a committee to coordinate their activities.[1]

In a telephone conversation with Assistant Secretary of State

Adolph Berle, Roosevelt stated, "The FBI should be responsible for foreign-intelligence work in the Western Hemisphere, on the request of the State Department," while "the existing Military Intelligence and Naval Intelligence branches should cover the rest of the world, as and when necessity arises."[2]

Under this directive, Roosevelt ordered J. Edgar Hoover, the head of the Federal Bureau of Investigation (FBI), to create a secret intelligence service to identify U.S. citizens and legal residents who might pose possible security risks for the United States. Because he was also concerned that the Nazis might establish operations in Central and South America, he authorized Hoover to set up a secret intelligence operation in Latin America. Even though the program was secret and illegal, on July 1, 1940, Hoover officially created the Special Intelligence Service (SIS).[3]

Heavily influenced by the hysteria of the American people and the excesses of the Justice Department's Enemy Alien Bureau during World War I, Hoover was prejudiced against foreigners. Starting in September 1936, he instituted a secret five-year plan to list all individuals who he believed posed a security risk to the United States. He ordered every agent to gather all information on these people regardless of the source or accuracy of the information.

Appearing before Congress in 1939, Hoover stated that the FBI had more than ten million individuals under surveillance, with a large number of those of foreign extraction. He further stated that the names were organized alphabetically and geographically so that if at any time America should enter into war, the FBI would be able to go into those communities and identify individuals and groups who might be a source of grave danger to the security of the country.

Some members of Congress were alarmed over Hoover's enormous power. Senator Kenneth McKeller of Tennessee tried to force him to disclose information about the FBI's secret activities, but Hoover refused. Instead he combined the list to produce the Custodial Detention Index (CDI). Broken down into three categories, the CDI listed everyone to be apprehended and interned immediately upon the outbreak of hostilities as well as those who were to be watched carefully. This included aliens who were leaders of non-political cultural organizations, individuals who were members of those organizations, and individuals who donated money to radi-cal pro-Nazi organizations or in any way indicated their support of those organizations.

Realizing that America might be dragged into the war in Europe, on June 29, 1940, Congress passed the Alien Registration Act (also known as the Smith Act).[4] The Smith Act made it illegal for anyone in the United States to advocate, abet, or teach the desirability of overthrowing the government. The law required all "enemy aliens" in the United States over fourteen years of age to file a comprehensive statement of their personal and occupational status and a record of their political beliefs.

Under the Smith Act, "enemy aliens" were further required to report any change of name, address, or employment to the FBI, and they were not permitted to enter federally designated restricted areas. Should an "enemy alien" violate any of the provisions of the Smith Act, they were subject to arrest, detention, and internment for the duration of the war. Within four months, a total of 4,741,971 aliens were registered.

Roosevelt had served as Assistant Secretary of the Navy under Woodrow Wilson and he was very much aware of the German sabotage campaign on American soil during World War I. There is no question that the sabotage campaign on American soil and the resulting damage fueled Roosevelt's decision to implement the mechanisms of internment and relocation of those he considered to be enemies of the United States. He didn't want to risk sabotage in sensitive areas, especially any more Black Toms, and he ordered his assistant Secretary of War, John McCloy, to implement the intern-ment order.

Even before the bombs stopped falling on Pearl Harbor, the president and the Justice Department implemented the provisions of the Alien Enemies Act of 1798.[5] This act permitted the appre-hension and internment of "aliens of enemy ancestry" by the U.S. government upon declaration of war or threat of invasion. It gave the president blanket authority as to the treatment of "enemy aliens," and civil liberties could be completely ignored. They were afforded no protections under this law and as a result were subject to govern-ment oppression during wartime.

Roosevelt took other actions during the next two days that were to have devastating consequences for those deemed to be "enemy aliens." On December 7, 1941, he issued Presidential Proclamation 2525[6] that authorized the arrest and detention as well as travel and property restrictions of individuals of Japanese ancestry presently living in the United States. On December 8, Roosevelt issued proclamation 2526[7] and 2527[8] authorizing the arrest and detention of those of German and Italian ancestry. In addition to the proclamations, a blanket presidential warrant authorized U.S. Attorney General Francis Biddle to use the FBI to implement the actions as stated in the proclamations.

A memo went out from FBI Director J. Edgar Hoover to all Special Agents in Charge.

TO ALL SACs:

MOST URGENT. SUPERSEDING AND CLARIFYING PREVIOUS INSTRUCTIONS RE: GERMAN AND ITALIAN ALIENS. IMMEDIATELY TAKE INTO CUSTODY ALL GERMAN AND ITALIAN ALIENS PREVIOUSLY CLASSIFIED IN GROUPS A, B, AND C, IN MATERIAL PREVIOUSLY TRANSMITTED TO YOU. IN ADDITION, YOU ARE AUTHORIZED TO IMMEDIATELY ARREST ANY GERMAN OR ITALIAN ALIENS, NOT PREVIOUSLY CLASSIFIED IN THE ABOVE CATEGORIES. IN THE EVENT YOU POSSESS INFORMATION INDICATING THE ARREST OF SUCH INDIVIDUALS NECESSARY FOR THE INTERNAL SECURITY OF THIS COUNTRY. ABOVE PROCEDURE APPLIES ONLY TO GERMAN AND ITALIAN ALIENS, AND NOT TO CITIZENS. ALL INDIVIDUALS ARRESTED MUST BE TURNED OVER TO NEAREST REPRESENTATIVE OF IMMIGRATION AND NATURALIZATION SERVICE.
(In Original Caps)

HOOVER[9]

The wholesale arrest of German and Italian civilians began in the early morning hours of December 8, three days before Germany declared war on America.

From New York City to Los Angeles, from Seattle to Miami, from Detroit to New Orleans, and as far west as Honolulu, federal agents knocked on doors to arrest "enemy aliens."

Fathers, mothers, and sometimes both parents were arrested, disappearing into the maze of government red tape and bureaucracy. Children were left to fend for themselves and ended up in orphanages or in the care of relatives and friends. Homes were ransacked and private property destroyed. Arrests were frequently based on nothing more than uncorroborated, hearsay evidence gathered by the FBI and other intelligence agencies.

In an article published by the German American Internee Coalition, Rudy Dimmling described the invasion of his grandmother's home by agents of the FBI.

> As retold to me by my mother and aunt, FBI agents came to their apartment in the middle of the night. They woke them from their beds and ransacked their apartment. The agents proceeded to question my grandfather and without notice, took him away. For several days my grandmother did not know his whereabouts, until she learned that he was being retained at Ellis Island. The irony of this is incredible since Ellis Island, known to twelve million immigrants as the "front door of freedom," was also a holding place for my grandfather as an "enemy alien" and a threat to the United States.[10]

Once the fathers were arrested, daily life for the families became a never-ending nightmare. During the 1940s, men were the primary wage earners and controlled the family finances. While the husbands went out to work, the wives stayed at home to care for the children and do domestic chores. A majority of the internees were immigrants who had resided in the United States for years, but had not yet received their American citizenship. Suddenly, and without warning, husbands were arrested and taken to unknown destinations.

Families had no idea where their loved ones were being held or what had happened to them. Communication with the prisoners was sporadic at best and they often didn't hear from them for weeks and sometimes months. By law, only "enemy aliens" could be interned, but with the approval of the Department of Justice (DOJ) and other government agencies, some family members joined them in the internment camps. These "voluntaries" typically included the mother who was more than likely a native-born American or a naturalized American citizen and their American-born children.

The Civilian War Assistance Unit of the INS was designated as the agency that would decide if wives and children would be allowed to join their husbands in the family camps. Each case was decided on an individual basis. The case of Hans Rens as shown in official correspondence is typical of how they were handled.[11]

September 16, 1943

Mr. Hans Rens
c/o Officer in Charge
Fort Lincoln Internment Camp
U.S. Immigration & Naturalization Service
Fort Lincoln, Bismarck, N.D.

Dear Sir:

You are informed that the application for reunion at a family internment facility of this Service with your wife, Johanne Rens, has been approved, and that arrangements will be made for such a reunion at Seagoville, Texas, within the near future. However, it is not known at this time exactly when such reunion will be affected. Mrs. Rens has been informed of the above and has been cautioned to make her arrangements accordingly.

You and your wife will be notified as soon as arrangements are made for your admission to Seagoville. We regret to inform you that your dog will not be admitted to the internment camp.

Very truly yours,

N. D. COLLAER
Acting Assistant Commissioner for Alien Control

Newspapers from coast to coast published articles and stories applauding the raids, and printed incriminating lists of names. Ominous headlines fanned the flames of paranoia, hysteria, and hatred that were spreading across America like a raging forest fire. Even the most popular comic strips of the day, such as *Wash Tubbs* and

Captain Easy,[12] went out of their way to showcase the violence against these "enemy aliens."

The government now faced a serious dilemma. Space was at a premium, and housing had to be found for the detainees awaiting their hearings. Prisoners were held in temporary custody in jails, hospitals, schools, hotels, and any other available place until the DOJ agreed to hear their cases.

The proceedings took place before a civilian hearing board. Detainees were subjected to harassment, intimidation, and hostile questioning by U.S. Attorneys and FBI agents. Many of the accused were semi-fluent in English and didn't understand the questions. They had no right to counsel, and they couldn't contest the proceedings or question their accusers.

The ninety hearing boards across the United States were made up of people who worked for a dollar a year. First the board would question an FBI agent as to the prisoner's guilt or innocence. They would then ask the prisoner a series of questions.[13]

- Are you so and so . . . ?
- Were you born in Germany?
- Have you any relatives in Germany?
- What year did you come to the United States?
- If you were called to fight in the Armed Forces of the United States, would you be willing to do so?
- If this country was invaded by an enemy, would you be willing to help defend it?
- Would you be willing to defend it even against Germany?
- Do you have a dislike for England?
- Have you ever made application for citizenship?
- Where do you work?
- Has your wife been ill?
- Did you ever send money back to Germany?

Eberhard Fuhr was only seventeen years old when he appeared before the board.

> These boards were made up of people at one dollar a year, I believe. Art (Jacobs) thinks his dad was permitted a witness, but in my case and what I know of others, witnesses were not permitted.

I was so shook up at seventeen walking into the hearing room that I am not sure how many people were in the room. I believe it was chaired by the U. of Cincinnati president and that there were about seven people in the room, one of which was an FBI agent who asked most of the questions. There were no witnesses on either side.

Prior to going in, the *Cincinnati Enquirer* stated that two brothers were arrested as dangerous aliens and would be given a hearing and interned. That was my brother Julius and me.

One question was whether I had stated five years previously that Hitler was doing a good job. That would have been in 1938 when I was twelve. Because I was cautioned very pointedly when sworn in about the hazards of untruth, I said that I couldn't verify that, but they kept insisting they wanted an answer, thus after that being restated several times, I was asked COULD YOU HAVE SAID THAT, to which I replied that I was capable of saying that.

I was also shown a 10 x 12 glossy of when I was twelve. They asked me if that was me in the center of a group at German American Day at Cincinnati's Coney Island. The U.S. and German flags were both evident in the picture. I was asked about singing in the Kinderkor conducted by Kapplehoff, and, of course, I did. Incidentally, Doris Day is Kappelhoff's daughter and she was in the Kor with me.

I was asked whether I indoctrinated fellow students, pictures on the wall of the house, fealty to the U.S. Did I also love Germany, my native land, and about cousins and relatives in Germany, one of whom was in the **HITLER JUGEND** to which I stated the fact that it was a Boy Scout troop.

Then I was asked, "If this cousin came up the Ohio River in a U-boat, landing at night, and knocked on my door for asylum, what would I do?" Well I knew geography enough and the famous "by the mark twain" that a U-boat would founder way down south on the Mississippi, much less reach the Ohio at Cairo. When I told them that, they realized how nuts the question was and they all seemed angry. Shortly after that, I was dismissed and returned to the Hamilton County Workhouse. The next day to Chicago and internment.[14]

At the conclusion of each hearing, the hearing board forwarded their recommendations to the Alien Enemy Control Unit (AECU) of the DOJ for a final determination that could take weeks or months. Detainees remained in custody waiting for the resolution of their cases: unconditional release, parole, or internment.

Based on the recommendations of the AECU, the U.S. Attorney General issued internment orders to hold the internees for the duration of the war. The orders tore families apart and destroyed lives. Family members who were left behind were shunned by long-time friends and neighbors. They feared that they, too, might be arrested or painted with the same "enemy alien" sentiments. Families became destitute and lost everything they owned. They were forced to apply to the Civilian War Assistance Unit for permission to join their spouses in family camps, apply for welfare, or seek aid from other family members who could afford to support them.

The government covered all the bases when on March 11, 1942, President Roosevelt signed Executive Order 9095 creating the Office of Alien Property Custodian.[15] This order gave the custodian discretionary and plenary authority over all alien property interest. When he froze their assets, he created an immediate financial catastrophe for affected families. According to the official records, much of the internees' confiscated property was sold for pennies on the dollar.

If the conditions the "enemy aliens" faced weren't bad enough, in the first two months of 1942, the government placed additional restrictions on them. With cooperation of the military, the DOJ established a network of restricted zones. "Enemy aliens" were forbidden to enter or remain in the designated areas, and their movements were closely monitored to ensure that they were in compliance. As can be imagined, such restrictions imposed tremendous hardships on those living and working in these areas.

More restrictions were placed on the prisoners when Roosevelt signed Executive Order 9066.[16] It authorized the Secretary of War to define military areas in which the right of any person to enter, remain, or leave should be subject to whatever restrictions were deemed necessary or desirable. This order applied to all "enemy" nationalities.

Congress ratified the order and placed even more stringent restrictions on the internees, authorizing the imposition of sanctions for violations of the order. They established extensive military zones on the East and West Coasts and in certain areas around the Great Lakes, and expanded the areas originally created by the DOJ.

Pursuant to the order, General John DeWitt issued a series of public proclamations creating Western Defense Command military areas.[17] The proclamations outlined curfews, travel restrictions, and exclusion provisions applicable to German, Italian, and Japanese aliens, as well as Japanese American citizens. This led to the exclusion of individuals and groups from military zones comprising over a third of the United States.

The government was particularly suspicious of naturalized citizens from enemy countries. On an individual basis, potentially dangerous U.S. citizens of German ancestry were ordered out of military zones and forced to establish new lives with little or no government assistance. The military threatened to exclude anyone they thought might pose a threat to the security of the United States. A large number of internees believed it was an exercise in futility to contest the exclusion order and left before they were forced to move.

Unlike group exclusions, the order required hearings for individuals selected for exclusion. In many ways, these hearings resembled the alien internment hearings. The accused were subjected to limited due process protections, clearly violating the rights of American citizens.

If an exclusion order was issued, excludees were given little time to leave the area. Homes were abandoned and families left behind. FBI agents followed them to their new communities and destroyed any chance they might have for a decent life. They advised police and employers as to how dangerous the excludees were. It became impossible for them to find suitable employment or housing.

Some excludees decided to fight. They took the government to court to contest their exclusion orders and to protest the government's violation of their due process rights. Numerous federal courts found the military's actions of questionable constitutionality and the program decreased in popularity. In lieu of exclusion, the government often sought to denaturalize American citizens so they could be interned as enemy aliens or deported back to their country of origin.[18]

NOTES

1. Franklin Delano Roosevelt, Presidential Directive, Administrative Records, SIS, RGCS, NACP, June 26, 1939.
2. Franklin Delano Roosevelt, telephone directive prepared by Assistant Secretary of State Adolph Berle and approved by the president, 24 June 1940, Section 2, File 64-4104, Administrative Records, SIS, RG 65, NACP,
3. Administrative Records, SIS, RGCS, NACP, June 26, 1939.
4. Alien Registration Act, Statute 670–71; Title I, 2–3, June 28, 1940.
5. Alien Enemies Act, July 6, 1798, 50 USC 21–24, 1918 Codification.
6. Franklin Delano Roosevelt, Presidential Proclamation 2525, Alien Enemies—Japanese, 6FR, 6234, 55 Stat 1703, December 7, 1941.
7. Franklin Delano Roosevelt, Presidential Proclamation 2526, Alien Enemies—German, 6 FR, 6324, 55 Stat. Part 2, December 8, 1941.
8. Franklin Delano Roosevelt, Presidential Proclamation 2527, Alien Enemies—Italian, 6 FR, 6324, Stat. 1707, December 8, 1941.
9. Directive from J. Edgar Hoover to all Special Agents in Charge, December 8, 1941.
10. Rudy Dimmling, *The Reseneder Family Internment Story*, German American Internee Coalition.
11. Family Camp Report, Civilian War Assistance Unit, September 16, 1943, *Freedom of Information Times*.
12. *Washtubs* and *Captain Easy* cartoons, Newspaper Enterprise Association.
13. Arthur Jacobs, email to author, March 19, 2009.
14. Eberhard Fuhr, *My Internment by the U.S. Government*, 2008.
15. Franklin Delano Roosevelt, Executive Order 9095, creating the office of Alien Enemy Property Custodian, March 11, 1942, 7 F.R. 1971, as amended by Executive Order 9193, July 6, 1942, F.R. 5205.
16. Franklin Delano Roosevelt, Executive Order 9066, authorizing the Secretary of War to prescribe Military Exclusion Areas, Section 4, Act of April 20, 1918, 40 Stat. 533, as amended by Act of November 30, 1940, 54 Stat. 1220, and the Act of August 21, 1941, 55 Stat. 655 (USC, Title 50, Section 104), February 19, 1942.
17. "Evacuation to Be Carried Out Gradually," *San Francisco News*, March 2, 1942.
18. Memo, War Department, *Suits for Cancellation of Naturalization against Subjects of Individual Exclusion Orders*, December 2, 1942.

THREE

MAX EBEL, A GERMAN IMMIGRANT'S STORY

Recounted by Karen Ebel for her father, Max Ebel Jr.

M ax Ebel, a U.S. resident German alien, was interned from September 1942 until June 1944. The reason for his internment was never explained to him. During the time he was interned, he was in five different internment facilities and worked for the Northern Pacific Railroad in North Dakota. This is his story.

Max Ebel was born in Speyer, Germany, on June 1, 1919, the second child of Max Ebel Sr. and Wilhemina Lehr. His father was a master carver and sculptor, an excellent musician, and a decorated World War I veteran. His workshop was at his home in Speyer. Growing up, Max also learned the trade and apprenticed to another master carver. Max belonged to the German version of the Boy Scouts and later the Red Cross.

The years after World War I were very difficult, and like many Germans, the Ebel family struggled. Max Sr., a bit of a "bohemian artist," became estranged from his wife and answered the call of a friend to do stone work on the National Cathedral in Washington, DC. He left Wilhemina and three young children in September 1929, looking for a better life. Max remembers that was the year the Rhone River froze, a very rare occurrence. Max never saw his dad again until he came from Boston to visit in 1936 with his new wife. At that time, he was already a naturalized United States citizen.

With the German economy on the rocks, things only got worse for the family left behind. They were virtually destitute, and Hitler's thugs started to take hold of the country. Max got rickets from malnutrition. Some of his happiest memories were of his time with the Boy Scouts and the Red Cross.

He wanted nothing to do with the Hitler Youth and steered clear of it. Max was always a pacifist. He couldn't explain why but thought it stemmed from his father's wartime experiences. Max Sr. fought in hand-to-hand combat in France and was forced to kill a man to avoid being killed himself. Every year for days leading up to the June anniversary of this event, he became sullen and depressed.

Late in 1936, all boys were required to join the Hitler Youth. Max's boys' organizations were merged into Hitler Youth. Max refused to join and came under increasingly hostile pressure from young nationalistic teenage boys. In early 1937, this culminated in a knife fight with another boy, a member of the Hitler Youth. As the crowd cheered for their Hitler Youth comrade, Max was stabbed in the hand. He grabbed the knife and slashed the other boy's face. Max escaped, but life in Speyer became too dangerous for him. He needed to get out. He was seventeen.

A decision was made. He would join his father in America. Max Sr. had established a woodworking shop in Cambridge and could use his help. Max went through a hasty procedure to obtain his passport. Riding his bike back and forth to Stuttgart was no small feat. Wilhemina signed the document permitting him to leave, and his boss wrote a letter of recommendation. Max left Germany from Hamburg in May 1937 on the SS *New York* bound for New York City. He had a German nickel in his pocket, a suitcase filled with his woodworking tools, a new wool suit, shoes, a shirt, and his coat. He never saw his mother again.

After a week-long voyage, he arrived in New York Harbor on a hot day. His father was waiting for him, and they walked from the harbor to the train station. Max was struck by how dirty the city was. On June 1, he celebrated his eighteenth birthday with his father in Boston. Max recalls, "I was an American right from the beginning, and I always will be. I think I appreciated my freedom as much as a fish let out of a bowl to swim in a river." That freedom was short-lived, however. The very influence Max had fled Germany to escape had followed him in the form of a cloud of suspicion. "I left Germany because of the Nazis, and I came over here and was treated like a Nazi," he said.

Max was happy working with Max Sr. in Cambridge. He befriended a fellow employee, an African American named Johnny who taught him English. And he taught Johnny German. Max joined the Boy Scouts and went to school to study to become a United States citizen. Later he became a Junior Air Raid warden and lived among other German immigrants in a large, socially active German American community in the Boston area.

Max Sr. was a very popular man who frequently served as the master of ceremonies at many area picnics and dances in German American clubs. As was common with immigrant communities, German diplomats mingled frequently with the community, as well as seamen from ships docking in Boston harbor. Max Sr. was also a member of a German World War I veterans' group of about ten men who met at each other's homes to play cards and enjoy each other's company. They took turns being president of the nonpolitical organization, which had limited ties to the World War I veterans' group in Germany, the Kyffhauser Bund. The group raised funds and existed pursuant to a permit issued by the Secretary of State. The money primarily went to widows and orphans of World War I veterans. Whatever it might have been in Germany, and how the money may have been divided up, for Max Sr. it was a social organization like so many veterans' associations.

Max remembered how much fun it was to tour a German freighter, the Pauline Friederich, impounded in 1939 after Germany invaded Poland. The tour was arranged by the first mate, who was an old school friend of Max Sr.'s from Speyer that he hadn't seen in years. Several of the German seamen later had dinner at Max Sr.'s home.

During this time, Max was also getting letters from Germany demanding that he return to serve in Hitler's army. Max burned the first two letters. When a third arrived, Max Sr. took him to the consulate where they persuaded the consulate to strike his name from the rolls. Max refused to return to Germany to fight for something he did not believe in.

The Ebels didn't know it, but the FBI was watching them and many others in Boston's large German American community. Years later, researching her father's internment story, his daughter Karen learned that the FBI knew of the visit to the boat, Max Sr. hosting the dinner at his home for the seamen, and their visit to the consulate. The FBI had a picture of him leaving the consulate with his father. Max was later relieved of his volunteer duties as an air raid warden. He never knew why, but he was hurt and disappointed. He enjoyed the work and the chance to help his newly adopted country.

The Ebels' Cambridge Woodcraft Company continued to make fine furniture. Amazingly, under the circumstances, they secured a contract with the United States Navy designing and building lifeboats that wouldn't overturn or sink. Max filed his Declaration of Intention to become a U.S. citizen on December 5, 1941.

After the Japanese bombed Pearl Harbor, life changed drastically for Max. President Franklin D. Roosevelt immediately issued the necessary Presidential Proclamations pursuant to the Alien Enemies Act declaring all Japanese, German, and Italian aliens to be "enemy aliens" and placing them under the jurisdiction of the Department of Justice. Along with over one million resident aliens, Max had to register at the local post office, be fingerprinted, and carry a picture ID. No enemy aliens were allowed to have radios, cameras, or firearms, and their travel was severely restricted. Max's citizenship plans stopped and he registered with the Selective Service. When asked if he would fight for the U.S. in Germany, he said no. He did not want to fight against his cousins, brother, and friends in the land of his birth. He was classified 4C.

Sometime in August 1942, armed FBI agents searched the Ebel home twice. A presidential warrant had been issued after Pearl Harbor, authorizing searches of homes in which an enemy alien such as Max resided. One time Max told the officers about a secret compartment in the nightstand he'd designed. They stood with guns drawn as he unlatched the hook and opened the compartment. They left the Ebel home with Max Sr.'s radio and camera, as well as various German language books and a calendar. Even though he was an American citizen, nothing was ever returned.

On September 21, 1942, Max Sr. was served notice by the army that he was to appear at a hearing on September 25 to show cause why he should not be excluded from the Eastern Military Area due to military necessity. Max Sr. was questioned at length without an attorney and returned home. On September 28, Max, then twenty-three, was picked up from work for questioning. He never returned home. He was sent to the Boston immigration station where he remained with other German and Japanese detainees for three months. He was permitted limited visitation rights and very little exercise. The few reading materials available had everything about the war cut out. He was never told why he was there.

Sometime during the next few weeks, Max was sent for his internment hearing. He had no counsel and no right to question the proceeding. He was permitted two character witnesses, and his father attended the brief hearing. Max recalls it lasting about fifteen minutes. He hardly spoke. The civilian hearing board was comprised of three local appointees. The district attorney chastised Max and laid out "evidence" against him as did investigating FBI agents. The primary objection Max recalls is that he didn't want to fight in Germany. The attorney told him that if his own son could fight, then Max could damn well fight too. He also told Max that it was his pleasure to fight Germans in World War I. Max returned to his cot at the immigration station.

Max remembered many things from his time of being detained in Boston. One incident in particular caused him great difficulty. One day he heard water running in the toilet room. A fellow German detainee, a doctor, yelled for Max. An elderly Japanese man was hanging over the toilet, slashed on either side of his neck, a jagged razor on the floor. They saved his life. He returned later with a cloth around his neck.

The man worked six days a week for a local family. On his day off, he went to have his shoes shined at a place that happened to be across the street from the GE plant. He was detained because the FBI thought he was a spy.

Another Japanese man gave Max a rosary with a crucifix that opened to disclose a small compartment that could hold a relic or some other holy object. The man told Max he could take the rosary—all that Christianity had done for him was to get him in trouble. The FBI assumed he was using it to smuggle microfilm. Max was also detained with a member of the Hapsburg family. A local women's club gave the men Christmas songbooks because they spent Christmas in the immigration station.

Max remembers waiting for his hearing with a very anxious German man and his wife, whose face was covered with red sores. The woman was sent to the local Home of the Good Shepherd run by Catholic nuns. The man, Mr. Groh, later joined Max and signed his songbook.

Finally, on January 20, 1943, Max was advised that he was being moved immediately to Ellis Island, along with several others. The Alien Enemy Control Unit of the Department of Justice, headed by Edward Ennis (later head of the ACLU), did not accept the parole recommendation of the hearing board and Attorney General Francis Biddle ordered him interned. With no notice to anyone, Max was put on a train and sent to Ellis Island.

Ellis Island was the dirtiest, most crowded place he was held during his internment. Hundreds of German men were packed into a huge room. The only source of privacy came from blankets hung from a top bunk. Max was glad to have a bottom bunk. The food was terrible and the medical care nonexistent. Infrequent exercise was made available outside behind barbed wire fences overlooking the Statue of Liberty. Lady Liberty seemed to mock the immigrants she invited to her shores. Max became ill and was refused medical care "because he was being shipped out the next day." And so he and many other German internees continued their journey to Fort Meade, Maryland.

The trip from Ellis Island to the mainland was difficult. The men were transferred to military custody. The soldiers were hostile and pointed their guns menacingly at the prisoners. The captain screamed that he didn't care if they went to Fort Meade "upright or feet first." Once they got to the New Jersey shore, they had to line up and the civilians stared at them. Max thought everyone was told that they were prisoners of war. When they got into the train, the shades were drawn and the windows were nailed shut. Soldiers were in every car with their rifles.

Max was at Fort Meade for about two weeks. He didn't mind

the stay. He got medicine for his severe sore throat and ate well, thanks to the German cooks interned there from New York City. Even the soldiers enjoyed their cooking. He got a physical and vaccinations before moving on to Camp Forrest in Tullahoma, Tennessee on February 24, 1943. The internees were taken there in a shuttered train under guard, although the shades were lifted in some of the more rural areas. Max remembers stopping somewhere along the trip through the Appalachians and seeing some of the locals in the forest.

Camp Forrest was run by the army, and rumor had it that a German internee was shot dead by a nervous camp guard before they got there. At Camp Forrest, there were quite a few prisoners. They lived in five- or six-man huts with the windows painted black and surrounded by muddy ditches to contain rainwater.

Max always wanted something to do and signed on to help the military doctors treat internees. He had a good relationship with the doctors, and when the internees were being shipped out to make room for German POWs, they wanted him to come with them but were not able to work it out. Max was disappointed.

In late May 1943, the men were shipped to a variety of camps, most of them to Fort Lincoln in Bismarck, North Dakota. They were once again taken by rail under guard with the shutters down in populated areas. Ironically, Max's first cousin who had been drafted into Hitler's armed forces arrived at Camp Forrest as a German POW shortly after Max's departure.

Fort Lincoln, now the United Tribes Technical College, was a United States Army fort that had been turned over to the INS for male internees. Located a few miles south of Bismarck in a very flat, barren area, Fort Lincoln reportedly consisted of approximately ten acres surrounded by a ten-foot-high wire fence buried three feet in the ground. It was topped with three strands of barbed wire, floodlights, and guard towers at regular intervals. Some sections of the fence were hooked up with microphones that broadcast at the slightest touch. Guards with dogs patrolled the perimeter.

Winter in North Dakota was brutal. Max arrived there exactly six years after arriving in the United States. He kept a small diary from his internment in which very little is written besides the dates of his transfers. Upon his arrival in Bismarck, he wrote, "This is hell."

The men lived either in brick buildings with large rooms holding many beds or in smaller temporary barracks. They were expected to help with the functioning of the camp, and Max served in the kitchen peeling potatoes many times. He hated being behind barbed wire and still had no idea why he was being incarcerated. He wanted out.

In September 1943, he got his chance. The Northern Pacific Railroad was looking for help because most of the able-bodied men in the Dakotas had enlisted in the military. The U.S. government worked with the German government and eventually the men were cleared to work with the railroad. The camp officials requested volunteers and five hundred men signed up. The list was eventually whittled down to about a hundred, and Max was one of them. The men were to replace existing rails that would accommodate wartime munitions traffic across the country. Some of the prisoners perceived this as helping the U.S. war effort, and they bitterly opposed the men who had agreed to help their "jailors." It made life uncomfortable for the volunteers for a time.

On September 3, 1943, Max and over one hundred other volunteers left Fort Lincoln and arrived in Buffalo, North Dakota, to begin work on the railroad. They lived in boxcars, six to eight men to a car heated by a coal stove. Water was held in a tank car at the rear of the train. There were no bathroom facilities besides the great outdoors. Max only returned once or twice to Fort Lincoln. It was a rough existence, but Max preferred it to living behind barbed wire.

Max worked with other men on the spike puller. The train was stationed in various towns, and the men were allowed to go into the towns under some observation and visit the restaurants, where they got to know the townspeople. Max greatly appreciated this bit of normalcy.

The train had to work on a spur in the Standing Rock Indian Reservation. During this time, the men met many of the Lakota who sold them handmade items off their buckboards. With great sadness and amazement Max recalled their abject poverty.

Once he looked inside one of the huts the families lived in and was surprised to see dirt floors. The Indians had pulled up the floors for firewood to keep warm. The men attended church on the reservation near Cannonball. At one service, the minister begged the men for money to help replace the church roof. The internees didn't have much, but they donated what little money they had earned working on the railroad. Later they were invited to attend Christmas Eve service and have dinner at the church.

During the festivities, which Max enjoyed greatly, the internees learned of a ten-year-old Indian girl who was dying of TB. The U.S. government hadn't provided sufficient health care, so the men contributed a few dollars to help save her. A kinship arose between these two outcast communities—Native Americans and German internees. Max would remember those times fondly all of his life. It was something good that came out of his internment.

One internee, Karl Klein, took responsibility for his fellow railroaders and continually implored the Department of Justice to review their cases in the hope of winning release. Finally, the DOJ agreed to hear their cases. The release recommendation of the rehearing board stated that the board questioned why Max had ever been interned. When this document was obtained from the National Archives in 1999, it was the first summary Max had ever seen of the original rationale for his internment. He had never seen the recommendation before.

At about the same time as the rehearing, Max was sent without a guard to Fort Snelling, Minnesota, for a pre-induction physical by the U.S. Army. Max found this ironic. He was considered so dangerous that he was interned, but was deemed trustworthy enough to fight for the United States in the war. Max flunked his physical and never joined the army.

In June 1944, Max was paroled and returned to Boston where he had to report to his parole officer once a week. He was not allowed to go near the railroad or subway lines, which always rankled him considering that he helped build them while interned. Finally, his parole was terminated in November 1945, and the nightmare of the past four years ended. After internment, he returned to work for his father, met Doris Eckert, and married her in October 1948.

Max became a United States citizen in 1953, twelve years after filing his intention to become a citizen. His citizenship application was intensely scrutinized because of his internment. He recalls the folders brought by the government to a related review as being "a mile high." He told them that they seemed to know more about him than he did. In a way, this was true. Max passed away in May 2007, never fully understanding why he was interned.

FOUR

THE LATIN AMERICAN CONNECTION

Early in the war, United States government policies toward Central and South America were driven by concerns for national and hemispheric security, economic control of Latin American markets, and disposition of "enemy aliens" in Latin America. President Roosevelt was concerned that Nazi agents would become established in Central and South America. He ordered Hoover to surreptitiously place his agents in sensitive locations throughout the Southern hemisphere. They posed as legitimate businessmen or legal and civilian attachés in embassies and consulates.

Despite the fact that many of these agents were poorly trained and unable to read, write, or speak Spanish, German, or Japanese, they did have some major successes. They tracked down the clandestine radio stations German agents used to send sensitive wartime intelligence back to their handlers in the motherland. The intelligence covered everything from Allied activities, to troop and supply movements in major ports and airstrips, to political gossip.

The list of Special Intelligence Service (SIS) operations in Latin America is long and varied. Between 1941 and 1945, SIS Agents seized enemy radio stations and arrested their operators in almost every Latin American country. One of their more successful operations was a campaign to stop Axis agents from smuggling platinum out of Colombia and shipping it back to Germany. Desperate for platinum, the Germans were ready, willing, and able to pay top dollar. Once in their possession, German agents smuggled the precious metal overland into Axis-friendly Argentina and loaded it on ships bound for Europe.

Using local residents and informers, SIS agents hiked through the jungles of Colombia searching out and destroying smuggling trails. Between 1942 and 1944, SIS agents monitored the production of platinum in Colombia and were able to account for all but 2,507 troy ounces mined during that period. It isn't known if the missing metal fell into German hands, but it's an insignificant amount when compared to the 137,500 troy ounces the German military needed.[1]

The second reason the United States intervened in the affairs of Central and South American countries was economic control of Latin American markets. They believed that controlling Axis-owned businesses would block the flow of profits to the enemy to help finance the German war effort. They reasoned that it would also eliminate competition with American companies.

On July 17, 1941, Roosevelt signed Presidential Proclamation 2497,[2] *The Proclaimed List of Certain Blocked Nationals, People, and Businesses the United States Will no Longer Deal with Economically.* This proclamation effectively prevented U.S. companies from doing business with them, and it opened the door for U.S. businesses to take over the blacklisted companies.

Perhaps the most important reason for U.S. intervention in Latin America was the need to gather captives as bargaining chips to barter with Axis countries holding American prisoners. With the approval of the president, the State Department implemented the Latin American Internment Program. An internal State Department memo of November 3, 1942, pulled no punches when it outlined the purpose of the program and how they planned to trade harmless detainees in exchange for allied citizens held in Axis countries.

It is particularly desirable that the repatriation of inherently harmless Axis nationals may be used to the greatest possible extent in obtaining the repatriation from Axis territories of Nationals of the other American Republics whose presence in enemy territory gives the enemy a certain amount of bargaining power.[3]

In a State Department document dated February 6, 1941,[4] Assistant Secretary of State Adolph Berle labeled many Latin-American

German groups as subversive, indicting German commercial firms as "indispensable media for the operation of the Nazi system, and asserting that . . . virtually all the Reichsdeutschen (Germans born in Germany) in Latin America are sincere supporters of the Nazi regime. Virtually every non-Jewish German citizen belongs to some branch of the Nazi hierarchy." Berle called for all ambassadors and consular officers to report any suspicious German individuals and German commercial firms. The document was coded as strictly confidential and sent to all Latin American embassies for action.

Ambassadors and other government officials were urged to apply pressure on Latin American governments to arrest and intern their citizens from Axis countries. They were to do it in such a way that their actions could not be traced back to the United States. The U.S. Embassy in Costa Rica sent a written memo to the Costa Rican Foreign Office listing the names of people approved by the Alien Enemy Control in the U.S. for deportation and internment in the U.S.[5]

A conference of ministers of friendly Western Hemisphere countries was held in Rio de Janeiro January 15–28, 1942.[6] To push its Latin American Internment program, the U.S. pressured its allies to create the Emergency Advisory Committee for Political Defense. Its main purpose was to impose the same restrictions as those in place in the United States. Other restrictions included slowing down naturalization procedures so aliens could not become citizens. Arrest and detention, as well as cancellation of citizenship of any native-born or naturalized citizen who supported the Axis powers in any way were recommended. Reports poured in from sources generally thought to be reliable on people believed to possess Nazi sympathies. The stage was now set for the arrests, imprisonments, and deportations that followed.

Through secret arrangements and financial support, thousands of legal residents of German, Italian, and Japanese ancestry residing in Central and South America and the islands of the Caribbean were arrested and held in detention centers without hearings or legal recourse. An unknown number of prisoners were shipped directly to Germany, Japan, or Italy.

Conditions under which the detainees were held varied from country to country. Some detainees were held in the U.S. military compounds, such as Camp Empire in Balboa in the Panama Canal Zone, or in the U.S. funded prison on Isle of Pines in Cuba. Some countries used local prisons and penitentiaries to house their prisoners. If the detainees had wealth and connections, they could buy accommodations in a hotel or, as in Ecuador, simply move away from the coast to inland areas. By December 1942, the State Department had decided to bring the detainees to the United States for temporary internment.

In response to a letter from the Commanding General of the Caribbean Defense Command, General George C. Marshall listed specific instructions for the final disposition of internees from certain South American countries. His memo of December 12, 1942, restated the State Department's intended purpose for the internees that "these interned nationals are to be used for exchange with interned American civilian nationals."[7]

Deportation to the United States was utter chaos. The U.S. government had assembled a large assortment of military ships and privately owned vessels to transport the prisoners and their families to ports in the United States. All baggage, money, passports, and visas were confiscated. When luggage was returned to the deportees at their point of debarkation, they found that it had been rifled and many of their possessions stolen.

Heidi Gurcke Donald was just seven years old when her family was deported from Costa Rica to the United States. In her story published on the German American Internee Coalition website, she describes the deplorable shipboard conditions she and her family and other deportees were forced to endure.

> Around January 20, 1943, we women and children were herded onto a train with the men, late at night so we would not be seen, and taken to Puntarenas, the Pacific port, where officials gave the children canned milk, the first food in the long trip. Most of us, already queasy from the trip, vomited it immediately. Launches took us in groups out to the ship, the USAT *Puebla* where passports and visas were confiscated. Each of my parents was allowed to take $50 (U.S.). Costa Rica kept all the rest of our funds. The men and teenage boys were taken to the hold. The women and children were crowded into cabins. For a week, the

ship sat in port in blackout conditions. For a week, until the ship sailed on January 26, no one was allowed on deck. No portholes could be opened. It was hot and humid, and soon the air reeked of dirty diapers and old sweat. Most of the children, including my sister and me, were sick by now, feverish and fussy. Diarrhea and stomach upsets were common. Diapers had to be washed by hand and hung around the cabin to dry.[8]

The original arrangements for meals proved to be totally unworkable and had to be changed. Overstressed mothers had fifteen minutes to feed their cantankerous children and themselves, and some of the women went hungry. After the first failed attempt at some semblance of order, children were kept below and fed after the mothers had eaten. Some of the men were brought out of the hold to serve as waiters.

Armed guards circled the dining room to prevent the men from communicating with their wives. The women circumvented the guards by pretending to talk among themselves in Spanish or German. The men listened intently and were able to learn how their families were getting on under such harsh conditions. They were also able to take messages about their families to the prisoners in the hold.

Women and children suffered serious health problems from poor sanitation, confined quarters, and overcrowded cabins. By the time the *Puebla* docked at Terminal Island at San Pedro, California, children and adults had blistering, crusted-over sores on their faces, hands, and arms that oozed a thick yellow puss. Many more were sick with severe coughs and high fevers.

Conditions on other ships were as bad as or worse than the *Puebla*. Crew members were unprepared for the large number of women and children among the deportees. The host of passengers quickly overwhelmed inadequate sanitary facilities. Not much bigger than oversized closets, the cabins overflowed with aunts, cousins, mothers, and overactive runny-nosed children. Every available inch of steel deck was covered with bare mattresses, and wet diapers were hung everywhere.

The *Acadia*, with cabin space for 200 passengers, took on board a total of 675 Axis nationals from Peru, Ecuador, and Colombia on its northward journey, resulting in "unimaginable overcrowding," food shortages, and a lack of bathing facilities. When the USAT (United States Army Transport) *Colonel Frederick C. Johnson* sailed from Peru, women and children were assigned bunks without guardrails, in tiers of four in an approximately fifty by forty space. There was only one latrine for use by all prisoners, and the women and children had to go through the men's holding area to get there. Inadequate water supplies meant no water for bathing or washing, and drinking water was unavailable for much of the night.

Deportees arriving from Latin America disembarked at the Immigration and Naturalization (INS) quarantine stations at Algiers, Louisiana, and Terminal Island, San Pedro, California. The story of the USAT *Cuba* and its passengers is typical of the treatment the deportees experienced upon their arrival in the United States.[9]

The USAT *Cuba* arrived in U.S. waters at approximately 2:30 a.m. on March 21, 1944. As the ship proceeded up the Mississippi River to the INS station at Chalmette Slip in Algiers, customs inspectors, FBI and INS agents, and armed military personnel boarded the ship to process the passengers. On board were 540 German and Japanese aliens, including a number of children between the ages of five and fourteen. All male adults were housed in the two holds. The women and children occupied cabins on the upper decks.

Before customs operations began, an announcement in English, German, and Spanish was distributed among the passengers. It outlined the procedures for clearance of the ship to be implemented by government officers. In this way the deportees knew what to expect once they disembarked.

Customs examinations began with the male adults, followed by the women and children. Some of the passengers had more luggage than the hundred pounds they were allowed, and it caused a few problems for them. Customs agents rifled through their baggage, confiscating any item they considered contraband. Examinations lasted until 10:00 a.m. when the ship docked at Algiers.

Since the aliens came from an area infected with typhus, they were required to submit to a disinfestation process. Located just off the pier, the path to the plant was marked off by ropes and guarded by military police. Everyone on board the *Cuba* had to submit to the process before they were allowed through the checkpoint.

The deportees were brought off the ship in groups of seventy-five, but thirty of the men were left on board to clean up the ship and unload the baggage. The first group consisted of males over eight years old, followed by women, girls, and male children under five. It didn't take long for the men to pass through the plant, but the women and children required much more time than the men. After the long voyage, the children were difficult to handle and hard to control. Undressing and dressing the children was a major task in itself.

Before entering the plant, each person was required to disrobe and place all of his or her clothes into a mesh bag. They entered a large room where they showered under extremely hot water. Following the shower, they entered another room where a medical attendant sprayed them with a disinfectant. In the drying room, they donned their clothes and headed for the State Department checkpoint.

The aliens' clothes were kept in a large gas chamber and disinfected for forty-five minutes followed by blasts of strong air pressure to blow the gas out of the clothes. The deportees' baggage went through a similar process until it was discovered that the gas chamber was inadequate to handle it. The remainder of the baggage was sprayed with disinfectant powder as it sat on the pier.

As the prisoners passed through the control point, the name of each passenger was checked and the amount of baggage recorded. Each prisoner was given luggage tags according to their destination and an identification card to be attached to their lapels. The identification card listed name, destination, train number, and Pullman accommodations. Once through the control point, the prisoners tagged their bags and reported to the public health doctor to determine if they had any communicable diseases.

Two special trains were parked near the pier. As they were cleared through the control point, the deportees were directed to their train and car as indicated on their lapel ID card. The train destined for Crystal City, Texas, consisted of twelve Pullmans and two baggage cars. The train destined for Kenedy, Texas, was made up of five Pullmans and one baggage car.

For the first part of the trip, the two trains were combined into one long train. At the first stop in Avondale, Louisiana, they were separated. Two dining cars were added to the Crystal City train and one dining car to the train bound for Kenedy.

The Crystal City train arrived too late in the day to transfer the prisoners to the camp, so they were forced to spend the night onboard. In the morning they were unloaded from the train and marched under guard to their new home. It can be assumed that the same conditions prevailed for the deportees when they arrived at Kenedy.

At Crystal City, two Public Health Service nurses were on hand to greet the first group of 130 German women and children.[10] The nurses had organized a two-room dispensary and a contract dentist provided emergency care. They had their hands full until January 1943 when Dr. Symmes Oliver arrived in camp. He was followed a month later by a newly appointed dental officer. With the help of a German internee doctor, the staff initiated a program to train orderlies and nurse's aides.

In addition to the baggage the internees carried, they also brought a few contagious diseases with them. A medical crisis occurred when Dr. Oliver and his staff discovered fifty-five cases of whooping cough and eight cases of impetigo. Two children with acute medical needs required hospitalization at a local hospital. Most of the adults suffered from severe respiratory conditions that required immediate medical attention.

To avoid another crisis, Dr. Oliver ordered every internee who passed through the gates to be immunized. Since most of the infections originated with the Costa Ricans, he ordered them quarantined for the duration. He criticized the medical officer at San Pedro, California, for failing to quarantine these contagious prisoners and sending them on to a camp with no functioning hospital or even an isolation ward.

Dr. Oliver was in poor health when he accepted an offer to go to work for the Public Health Service. At fifty years old, he had hoped to find a less stressful situation before he retired, but the work may have been too much for him. It wasn't long before his coworkers and others complained about his heavy drinking and bouts of depression. They accused him of belittling and criticizing his staff. His detractors said that he showed poor leadership and his subordinates were forced to assume responsibilities that should have been his. According to his accusers, he instilled little confidence in either staff or patients by his hesitancy to make medical decisions and his refusal to perform surgery when needed.

The added responsibility of supervising a new fully equipped hospital and the ever-increasing number of families with health problems arriving daily put a major strain on Dr. Oliver and his staff. INS decided to replace him with the medical officer from the camp at Fort Missoula, but until the new doctor arrived, Oliver had to stay on. During the transition, a competent nursing staff and several internee physicians kept the medical situation under control.

NOTES

1. G. Gregg Webb, *New Insights into J. Edgar Hoover's Role,* CIA Government Library, Washington, DC.

2. Franklin Delano Roosevelt, Presidential Proclamation 2497, *Blacklisting 1,800 Firms for Aiding Germany or Italy,* Section 5(b) of the Act of October 6, 1917 (40 Stat. 415) as amended and Section 6 of the Act of July 2, 1940 (54 Stat. 714) July 17,1941.

3. State Department memo, *Regarding Activities of the United States Government in Removing from the Other Republics Dangerous Subversive Aliens,* November 3, 1942.

4. State Department memo *To the Chiefs of Diplomatic Missions in the Other American Republics,* February 6, 1941.

5. State Department memo *To Costa Rican Foreign Office,* November 24, 1943.

6. Lawrence Hass, "Nations to Meet in Rio," *Salinas Index Journal,* January 3, 1942.

7. Letter from General George C. Marshall to Commanding General, Caribbean Defense Command, December 12, 1942.

8. Heidi Gurcke Donald, *Gurcke Family Story,* 2006.

9. Report From Bannerman to Fitch, *Arrival at New Orleans of 540 German and Japanese Internees,* March 28, 1944.

10. Louis Frist, "Medical Care for Interned Enemy Aliens, a Role for the U.S. Public Health Service in World War II," *American Journal of Public Health,* October 2003.

FIVE

THE GURCKE FAMILY

Recounted by Heidi Gurcke Donald

O ur family was one of thousands in Latin America who were caught in the far-flung net cast by U.S. authorities seeking "the enemy" during World War II. My father, Werner Gurcke, and his brother, Karl Oskar, lived through World War I as children in Hamburg, Germany. Costa Rica was their chosen country—a place to be free and happy, to work hard and get ahead. It was supposed to be a place where war would not touch them again.

I learned part of this story from my mother, who, in her eighties, consented to let me interview her. The memories were so painful it took more than a month of visits, recording her recollections in fragments, one sentence at a time. My father never talked about any of it. He had to face not only the destruction of his own way of life, but also the distress of knowing his parents and youngest brother were living through another war in Germany. After his death, I found that he had saved numerous letters and governmental papers tucked away in a shabby manila folder at the back of an old filing cabinet in the garage.

In the 1920s, Karl Oskar moved to Costa Rica and married a native woman, Paulina Carlotta Vargas, known as Pany, and gained a stepdaughter, Hermida Jinesta. My father, who arrived in Costa Rica in 1929, married my mother, Starr Pait, an American in 1936. They made their home in San Jose where I was born.

The British Blacklist listing my father's name and business was published in August 1940, five months after I was born. My parents soon realized that the business my father loved and had worked so hard to build would be badly damaged, if not destroyed. He was the middleman, working with foreign manufacturers to supply goods like buttons, watches, umbrellas, and fabrics to local retailers.

My sister, Ingrid, was born on July 17, 1941, the same day that the U.S. President, in Proclamation 2497, declared some people to be on "The Proclaimed List of Certain Blocked Nationals." Werner and Karl Oskar were listed, as was Starr. The U.S. Blacklist destroyed what was left of my father's business.

After careful consideration, my parents bought a small finca (farm) in San Juan de Tibas, where they hoped to weather the war years. My father had worked in a business office since he was thirteen, while my mother had a post-graduate language degree. As my mother wrote to a friend, "If we had our own land with a vegetable garden and maybe some chickens and a cow (!), we could at least live well for the duration of the war. . . . I can't imagine myself as a lady farmer, or Werner as a gentleman one, for that matter. But we could always learn."

The government had frozen all of their financial assets by October. At Christmas that year, Starr wrote to her brother:

> At least up til now, no drastic measures have been taken against the Germans. Some property has been confiscated, like power plants and coffee plantations belonging to Germans. Germans were arrested for a short while, and house searching is going on. We have already been very thoroughly and rather humiliatingly searched, but we believe, pronounced innocent of firearms, dynamite, and propaganda leaflets. We don't believe the blacklist will be considered as a reason for internment since half of Costa Rica is on it.

In January 1942, my father had to register as a resident alien. By then, a secret memo had labeled him as "one of the most dangerous German nationals in the country" in a report using "a source generally reliable." He was one of thirty-five men so named. One of the methods used to acquire information about possible "enemies" was to tear a coupon out of the local newspapers where anonymous informants could list and send in names. (Reliable indeed!)

By February, their mail was being routinely censored. A censor reported the following excerpt from a letter Starr wrote to a friend:

> Right now he's [Werner] the chief cause of all my worry. He's still with me, thank God, but I can't help wondering for how long. A short time ago, 38 Germans, supposedly those belonging to the Nazi Party here were deported very quietly and suddenly. A large concentration camp is being built here too; for whom is the big question. We've done all we think of to help—gone to the American consul—I'm still an American, and have written to the government, stating our innocence of any conspiring against it. Werner has to have a special permit to travel, that is, to go from here to town or to friends out of town, etc. Now there's talk about our having to give up our radio and camera, which would be a sham, but we would gladly do it if that were all that would happen to us.
>
> Werner's business has of course been completely ruined. He's still winding up the last few affairs, but spends most of his time at home now, working here and helping me tend the babies. . . . Werner, of course, doesn't hear from his family in Germany anymore. They must be sick from worry about us.

Now my parents were dependent on the finca for most of their livelihood. They bought a cow to supply us girls with milk but didn't know how to coax it to produce. They picked coffee beans—hot, dirty work. Neither had ever gardened before, but they tried to grow vegetables and harvest fruit. They had no help and did all the house and garden work while caring for Ingrid and me. Electricity was available only part of the day. Diapers were washed and wrung out by hand. Baby food had to be made daily since there was no refrigeration. As my mother mentioned to a friend in a letter: "There aren't any cute little kitchens with mix masters and toasters and running hot water and washing machines, etc. Labor is labor and you can't run to the corner Piggly Wiggly [a grocery store chain] and get a can or two for supper."

And all that time, they were afraid. They had no idea what to expect next, and neither the Costa Rican nor the U.S. officials would tell them anything. Each denied responsibility for the situation, pointing instead to the other government. On July 4, 1942, Karl Oskar, Werner's brother, was arrested and jailed along with many other German men. Werner was placed under house arrest.

On the 15th, Werner was taken to the local jail where his brother and the other men were kept until being moved into the new "concentration camp" about a week later. There was no bedding, so my mother wrestled a mattress into and out of their little Opel for him. In a letter to her brother she wrote:

> July 17, 1942
> Dear Charles and Virginia,
>
> Since day before yesterday, Werner has been in the local penitentiary. For a week he had house arrest and we were happy. We haven't the remotest idea why they arrested him or what's going to happen to him and the many others there. And they won't let me see anyone to find out the charges against him or to do any explaining. Heidi wakes up at night screaming, 'Papi, Papi' and today is Ingrid's first birthday. . . . As you can see, my heart is breaking—with all my love, Starr

In December 1942, my mother, sister, and I were picked up by the Costa Rican police and taken to the German Club in San Jose that was used as a holding facility for the wives and children of the men in the concentration camp. My Tia Pany and Hermida were also there. No preparations were made for us. Starr was able to hire a horse and cart to have a baby crib delivered the next day, but she and most of the women slept as best they could on the floor, taking what comfort they could in having their children beside them. Sanitary facilities were overwhelmed. Diapers were washed out in the swimming pool. The women were kept at the club for about a week and then sent home because according to rumors, a ship that was to take us away hadn't arrived.

A few days before Christmas, much to everyone's surprise, the German men, all those "dangerous" alien enemies were furloughed from prison to spend Christmas with their families. By then, they'd been given word that we were all being deported. My mother had been able to find out from a sympathetic Costa Rican policeman that we were to be taken to the U.S. We had a week to prepare for our departure.

On January 2nd, my father went back to prison while my mother finished packing. A week or so later, we were again picked up and taken to the German Club where we waited another week under indescribably unsanitary conditions. Children, including my sister and me, developed conjunctivitis (pink eye) and runny noses. Around January 20, 1943, we women and children were herded onto a train with the men, late at night so we would not be seen, and taken to Puntarenas, the Pacific port, where officials gave the children canned milk, the first food in the long trip. Most of us, already queasy from the trip, vomited it immediately.

Launches took us in groups out to the ship, the USAT *Puebla*, where passports and visas were confiscated. Each of my parents was allowed to take $50 (U.S.). Costa Rica kept all of the rest of our funds. The men and teenage boys were taken to the hold. The women and children were crowded into cabins.

For a week, the ship sat in port in blackout conditions. For a week, until the ship sailed on January 26, no one was allowed on deck. No portholes could be opened. It was hot and humid, and soon the air reeked of dirty diapers and old sweat. Most of the children, including my sister and me, were sick by now, feverish and fussy. Diarrhea and stomach upsets were common. Diapers had to be washed by hand and then hung around the cabin to dry. Cabins were inspected, and once a sailor would not allow any of us up on deck because diapers cluttered the cabin. Mom was furious about that. Where were they expected to hang diapers? I can imagine her lying on those mattresses, damp with her children's urine, and then trying to bundle them up somehow so we could move around the cabin in the daytime.

My mother had one positive memory. She'd forgotten her comb. A sailor took his comb out of his pocket and gave it to her. His kindness overwhelmed her both then and so many years later when she recalled it for me. My father never spoke of his experiences on the ship, not even to my mother.

By the time the *Puebla* landed at the Immigration Detention

Station, Terminal Island, San Pedro, California (7:00 a.m. on February 6), many more children were fevered and coughing. The faces, hands, and arms of many children and some adults had blistering sores crusted with thick yellow exudates. Both Ingrid and I were very sick. Mom was also coughing. She did not remember any medical help being offered. The men were taken away; no one knew where.

In San Pedro, Immigration and Naturalization Service (INS) officials and the FBI interrogated my mother. All deportees were brought before an INS Board of Special Inquiry. That hearing had one point only. "These proceedings are for the purpose of determining your right to enter the United States." According to the official board record, no legal representation was allowed.

After a week of interrogations and hearings designed to prove that we Latin Americans were entering the country illegally, thereby allowing detention, we were put on a bus and driven to a railroad station. We had to tie identification numbers, pinned on baggage tags that listed our destination, to our clothing. Our tags read Crystal City, Texas. At the station, we boarded a train and began our trip. The windows were dirty; no one could see out or in.

Many of the children were now coughing so hard they had trouble catching their breath. Some of us began vomiting on the train as well, the result of the illness that had begun in Puntarenas. After two days and one night, we arrived in Crystal City, where a bus picked up our sick, exhausted families. We were driven through town past the statue of Popeye that the city fathers had erected outside the courthouse to mark their town as the "Spinach Center of the World" and into the barbed wire enclosure of the camp. Our arrival is noted in the camp records: February 12, 1943, at 3:00 p.m.

"This group arrived with forty cases of whooping cough and an epidemic of impetigo. Fortunately, the camp was not yet crowded, and it was impossible to isolate the entire party."[1]

Others can tell you about the heat—up to 120 degrees in the summer—and the cold. The winter we were there, snow was on the cactus and icicles hung from our roof, the first we'd ever seen. There were dust devils all summer, as well as scorpions, biting red ants, tarantulas, and rattlesnakes. In the winter, the mud was thick; the hospital in particular was surrounded with mud "practically up to the knees when it rained," and medical staff had to store extra, clean shoes and stockings inside the building to put on after they waded in and washed up.

There was a huge wire fence opposite our little house, with armed guards in watchtowers and brilliant lights at night blocking out most views of the stars and casting shadows through the curtains my mother made for our bedroom.

In July, Werner and Karl Oskar learned that Hamburg had been bombed repeatedly. An estimated thirty thousand to fifty thousand civilians were bombed in Hamburg, and the city was almost completely destroyed. Months later, they received a Red Cross message saying that their parents and youngest brother had survived.

My uncle must have been active in camp life while interned. But he, with others, preferred freedom to indefinite detention, even if it meant being sent to a war-torn country. Karl Oskar applied for repatriation to Germany for himself and his family as soon as it was offered. His request was granted, and he and his Costa Rican wife and daughter joined a group of German Americans and Latin Americans to be repatriated from Crystal City, sailing on the *Gripsholm* on February 11, 1944. It was many difficult years later before he and his family were able to return to Costa Rica.

Latin Americans were not given even the original cursory hearings offered Enemy Alien Program detainees in the U.S. It was over one and a half years after my father was first imprisoned before he received a hearing on the "evidence" that led to his arrest. The "evidence" leading to my father's arrest, loss of business, property, country, and freedom was: Werner and Starr were members in the German Club and he had been treasurer there during 1934–35. The German Club was a social club, actively anti-Nazi until 1940. He stopped attending when pro-Nazi members insisted on using the Nazi salute. He also belonged to a local mutual benefit society, the Unterstutzungverein, founded by Germans in Costa Rica in the early 1920s. It was completely non-political.

Before the war, Werner had contributed about five colones (one dollar) to another group, the Winterhilfe (Winter Help), a benefit for Germans in need of assistance. Evidently some of the money collected by that organization was used to fund Nazi Party work in Latin America. He also had a list of addresses from around the world, confiscated during an FBI raid on his office. The addresses were all business related, as FBI agents noted.

By this time, independent investigators had been sent to Latin America to check on the credibility of accusations made by U.S. Embassy officials and FBI agents. A young lawyer, James Bell, looked at the cases of all thirty-five of the Germans labeled "most dangerous" in Costa Rica, and found little or no evidence against most of them. FBI investigations of my mother showed no credible reason for her internment either, so we were released, with my father designated as an "internee at large." Government officials originally called it "relaxed internment" but decided that sent the wrong message. We could not leave the U.S.

We went to Santa Cruz, California, to my mother's family beach house in May 1944. My mother and her family were well known in the small community of Seabright, and we were treated with kindness and respect. Ingrid and I thought our new home was a palace. We had no memories of upholstered furniture or private toilets. In Crystal City, our house's inside furnishings, other than beds, were four wooden dining chairs, a table, and one wooden outdoor lounge chair. The toilet and bath facilities had to been shared.

Since we were not allowed a camera, neighbors took family pictures for us. We took long, long walks. My father in particular couldn't get enough of freedom, walking as far as he could, as often as he could. Because he spoke fluent Spanish, he found work immediately, supplying groceries to Mexican labor camps.

There were still upheavals and constant uncertainty. In August 1944, and again in April 1945, his draft classification was changed to 1A. Yes, my "most dangerous enemy" father had to register for the U.S. draft, even while imprisoned! Ramon Fernandez, his boss, intervened both times. He was able to convince the board that Werner's work was essential to the war effort so that his draft classification was changed to 2A.

In January 1945, we were suddenly ordered to move from the coast, an order rescinded without explanation several weeks later. In February 1946, my father received word that his enemy alien status was lifted; the same day he was issued an arrest warrant for entering the U.S. illegally, with threatened repatriation to Germany.

In 1946, Werner received a letter from his mother, the first news of his family since 1943. The news was terrible. Though sickly, Werner's younger brother, Ulrich had finally conscripted into the military. He was killed when a hand grenade exploded during training exercises in February 1945. He was twenty-five.

Werner's father, too, was dead, less than a month after Ullie, and just two months before Germany's surrender. Max refused to eat after Ullie's death, and he died of a "broken heart." Karl Oskar and his family were as well as could be expected, as was his mother, Frieda.

Eighteen Seabright neighbors signed a petition to the Immigration and Naturalization Service asking that Werner not be sent to Germany, and finally, after years of struggle, the arrest warrant was canceled and he was allowed to begin steps toward naturalization. It was only then that they felt secure enough to have another child, a son named Karl. My father became a U.S. citizen in April 1952.

NOTES

1. Joseph L. O'Rourke, *Historical Narrative of the Crystal City Internment Camp*, a report to W. F. Kelly, assistant commissioner for Alien Control Office, Immigration and Naturalization Service, Crystal City Internment Camp, RG 85, 101/161, 32, NA, 21.

SIX

TRANSIT CAMPS

As the number of arrests increased and the temporary detention centers became overcrowded, it soon became obvious that permanent facilities were needed. The enemy alien program was under the joint control of the Army and the Immigration and Naturalization Service (INS). By March 1942, it had been decided to implement plans to build a number of camps. The Army's Provost Marshall General (PMG) was ordered to construct nine permanent camps and one camp reserved only for families. Future plans called for fourteen additional camps to be built at a later date.[1]

INS already had a ready-made police force to guard the camps. Despite strenuous objections by Willard F. Kelly, the head of the Border Patrol, they transferred a number of officers from duty along the Mexican and Canadian Borders. The officers weren't too enthusiastic about guarding enemy aliens, but they remained at the camps for the duration of the war.

Each camp was designed with a particular population in mind. There were men-only camps, camps for single women and childless couples, and camps for entire family groups. Internees were held at Civilian Conservation Corps (CCC) camps, migratory worker camps, military bases, and National Park Service facilities.

Most of the aliens arrested on the East Coast were taken to Ellis Island for processing. Ellis Island was the ideal place to imprison them. Surrounded by water, it was easily guarded, could only be reached by boat, and had plenty of room for large groups of people. Even to this day, the dark years of Ellis Island from 1941 to 1948 still remain a closely guarded government secret. Many German Americans were locked up behind barbed wire and iron barred windows for three years after the war in Europe ended.

During the early years of the war, Ellis Island served as a transit center and detention camp and in later years as the final departure point for prisoners selected for deportation or repatriation. From there the deportees boarded the Swedish ships, SS *Gripsholm*, SS *Drottningholm*, SS *Winchester Victory*, and SS *Aiken Victory* for their one-way voyage to Europe.[2]

Ferryboats transported the internees from Battery Park in New York City. Once ashore, they walked through a long tunnel-like entryway into the main hall of the Ellis Island Reception Center. Before they were processed through the center, they were searched to ensure they weren't carrying contraband or restricted items.

The center housed a barbershop, a music room with a piano, a canteen, a store, a hospital, and bathrooms with long rows of showers, toilets, and washbasins. Prisoners ate their meals in the massive dining room located on the second floor. Families were assigned to individual quarters, but children were often separated from their parents. Children and single men slept in barrack-type halls.

"Sleeping arrangements left a lot to be desired," explained an unidentified internee as she related her experiences on Ellis Island.

> I was a young lady of nineteen when I was interned. The first few weeks were horrible. Our beds were saturated with urine from refugees who came from European countries. We were ten women at the time and we had to share one room. Later, rooms that had been offices were converted into living quarters. I was assigned Room #1. As for cleanliness, there were many roaches— big roaches. The food was good and bad, or shall I say the food was fair.[3]

Male prisoners were issued a pair of U.S. Army brogans, khaki socks, a shirt and pants, underwear, and red and black plaid jackets. The women were given standard issue for women in the army at that time. They also received $3.00 a month in government scrip to purchase additional items form the store and canteen. Internees who chose to perform maintenance jobs around the island received an additional ten cents an hour for their labor.

Lutheran ministers conducted religious services in German every other Sunday, and Catholic services were held whenever a German-speaking priest was available. Due to limited cooking and eating facilities, prisoners were required to eat in shifts, and the food was adequate. Movies, athletics, and other forms of entertainment were provided. A reading room and small library off the Great Hall contained six hundred books written in German and five hundred books in English donated by the German Red Cross, the YMCA, and private individuals.

The author of *The Prison Called Hohenasperg*, Arthur Jacobs, remembers his internment on the island.

> On February 27, 1945, I was imprisoned at Ellis Island, New York Harbor, New York. Just 23 days after my 12th birthday I was a prisoner under control of the United States Department of Justice's Immigration and Naturalization Service (INS). This was to be my first of two internment periods at Ellis Island. This first period of my imprisonment on the Island ended on April 29, 1945 when my family and I were transferred to the Crystal City, Texas, family internment camp. Oh happy day!
>
> Before I left the Island I experienced a new way of "life." Classes for children did not exist during my stay there. Each day was a no school day. According to the official record, formal school was conducted for school-age children on the Island, but it was not available to me. It was through an informal learning process that my education progressed on the Island. One of the first things I learned on the Island was that I was no longer an American. When I arrived on the Island, according to the INS classification, I was to become known as a German American. Yes, even though I was American, born in the U.S.A., the INS classified me as a German American. America is my country, I thought, and Germany, in my mind, was the enemy.
>
> Not only was my education interrupted, but also my social state of affairs was to undergo an abrupt and radical change. First, I was separated from my mother. Then, I was forced to live in an open bay with hundreds of males, some of whom had been

incarcerated since the war began in 1941. Privacy, there was none. Public wash basins, public toilets, public eating, public visitation—everything you did was in view of the public. If I was not being watched by the guards, I was being eyed by the inmates.

As I noted earlier, I was not quartered with my mother. My mother was quartered in another part of the island. Mom's quarters were in the Great Hall. During certain hours of the day, I could go visit my mother in the Great Hall. I could go to her room, but her and I could not visit there. We were required to visit in the downstairs portion of the Great Hall. Together, Mom and I would go downstairs into the open space of the Great Hall. Here we would sit down on a wooden bench, a little bigger than a love seat. We would chat about what I had been doing all day. My Mom was a stickler for details. Mom always insisted that I tell her everything. She would ask about my belt making. "What colors are you using for belts today?" Mom would ask and continue with another question, "Are you making narrow or broad belts?" And so it would go. Every now and then I would surprise Mom with a belt I made especially for her. Of course, Mom always wanted to know whether I was getting enough to eat. "Sure Mom," I would reply to her question. Our entire visit was always under the watchful eyes and the listening ears of the matrons and/or guards. I suppose no one wanted my mother and I to plot an escape.

Homesickness was a problem. Hour after hour, day after day, I would stare out across the water, view the Manhattan skyline, the passing ships, the puffing tugboats, the comings and goings of the U.S. Coast Guard Cutter and its crew members, whose duty station was Ellis Island. I want off this Island, was a constant thought which I kept to myself. "Why am I here?" I would ask over and over. My moods of nostalgia and melancholy would come and go. Reading would help overcome boredom. I read many western stories, mostly about the territory surrounding the Pecos River.

I remember talking to many of the adult male internees, asking them over and over again why they were there, and why they were there for so long. In February 45, when we had arrived on the Island, some of the internees I had spoken to had already been interned for more than three years.

After my first week or so, Island life had become somewhat routine. Out of bed at six o'clock in the morning, use the public latrine, wash my face, brush my teeth, clean up my living space, make my bed, dust from under my bed, and so forth. Then off to breakfast. Limited cooking and eating facilities required us to eat in shifts; say the first group at 6:30, the second at 7:00 and so forth. No special food orders. I ate what was put on my tray, a spoonful of this, and a spoonful of that ladled onto my metal tray. I cannot remember if the food was good or bad. What I was fed I do not remember.

On December 3, 1945, I was back on Ellis Island. My stay in the Crystal City (Texas) Internment Camp lasted only seven months. Seven months after the war in Europe had ended, we, my family and I, and hundreds of others, were still prisoners. This time, like my previous stay on the island, I was separated from my mother and was housed in an open bay with adult male internees. Since I left in April, the conditions on the Island had changed. It was more crowded and congested. There was little time and space for arts and crafts. It was a busy period for us. There were inoculations, physical examinations, and processing. It seemed like each day between the time we arrived on December 3 until we departed on January 17, 1946, we had to take care of some official transactions.

I was confused. I did not understand what was taking place. My most vivid memory of my second stay on the Island was how sore my arm was after being inoculated, smallpox vaccine, and one dose of typhoid vaccine. We were being prepared for a voyage to a war-torn and starving Germany. The scheduled time period between my first and second vaccine doses would occur after my departure date. Thus, the government decided that we could receive our second dose aboard ship while en route to Bremer-haven, Germany.

Before we left the Island, we celebrated both Christmas Eve and Christmas Day on Ellis Island. The officials did their best to make our stay comfortable. This was unlike any other Christmas I had ever experienced. For me it was both a day of sadness and a day of joy. It was a cold and dark December and January in the shadow of Liberty. On the 17th day of January 1946, I left the Island for the last time. We boarded a U.S. Coast Guard Cutter and were taken to the SS *Aiken*, a ship of the Victory Class. I was removed from my country. I would see neither the Statue of Liberty nor Ellis Island until 22 months later when I returned to my country in November 1947. The United States, what a beautiful sight to once again see the front side of Liberty.[4]

Ellis Island wasn't the only INS detention facility on the East Coast. Internees were held in a large Victorian mansion on South King Street in Gloucester City, New Jersey. Nicknamed the Ellis Island of South Jersey, it was located in an industrial area across the Delaware River from Philadelphia. It was used primarily as a transit camp for male and female detainees on their way to other more permanent locations. A passenger liner sailing between Florida and New England brought new prisoners in from the South every week. New internees arrived in groups of two or three at a time to await their appearance before a hearing board. After their hearings, some were released on parole or transferred to other internment camps.

The camp could house about four hundred internees, but there were usually no more than twenty to fifty detainees at any given time. There were a dozen cells in the basement for those thought to be dangerous or who might attempt to escape. Guards were unarmed and seldom had to deal with anything more dangerous than the occasional escape. At one point, thousands of gallons of confiscated whiskey were stored in the basement, but there is no record of prisoners breaking in to steal it.

Female internees were held for extended periods of time. Just as in the other camps, women received a dress and a pair of shoes. The men were issued shoes and a pair of sturdy work pants. Each internee was given one free pack of cigarettes each week. Prisoners earned eighty cents a day making handicrafts and were allowed to keep up to ten dollars. Any amount over the ten dollars was held in a special account.

In many ways, Camp Gloucester was a model camp. With so many large urban hospitals in the area, the internees had access to some of the best medical care available. To pass the time, they could participate in daily classes in Spanish and French. On Friday nights there were poker and gin rummy for the gamblers and Catholic or Protestant services for the religious on Sunday. They were permitted to have regular visitors, but message censorship and non-discussion of certain subjects were strictly enforced. Detainees had considerable freedom inside the facility, and there was an exercise yard along the banks of the Delaware River for those who wanted to take advantage of it. Crowds of tearful wives and children often gathered outside the camp for some word of their husbands or fathers who had disappeared in late-night raids.

While some of the detainees arrested during the early years of the war were confirmed Nazis, the majority of prisoners were aliens who had the bad luck to come under the scrutiny of the Justice Department. They may have done nothing more than make a careless remark, correspond with relatives in Germany, or be falsely accused by their neighbors.

One of the most famous and intriguing residents of Camp Gloucester was an Austrian immigrant, Princess Stephanie Hohenlohe-Waldenbourg-Schillingfust.[5] The U.S. government considered her the most dangerous spy in America. She resembled a character out of a cheap spy novel, and she was a mysterious femme fatale, an international playgirl who moved in the highest circles of European society. Everywhere she went, an air of intrigue surrounded the princess. She was a confidante of Fritz Weidman, a close friend of Adolph Hitler, and a former German Consul General at San Francisco. She apparently met the Führer several times and was acquainted with the hierarchy of the Nazi Party.

The French, British, and American governments suspected Princess Stephanie of being an international spy for the German government. They described her as being extremely intelligent, dangerous, and clever; an espionage agent worse than ten thousand men, reputedly immoral and capable of resorting to any means to gain her ends.

The government had been trying to deport the princess even before America entered the war, but no country would accept her. She was living in Philadelphia and was one of the first enemy aliens arrested and transported to Camp Gloucester. When local reporters visited the camp a few days after Pearl Harbor, they found confusion and sadness among the prisoners. Everyone, that is, except Princess Stephanie.

The press described this woman of glamour and international intrigue as the "jauntiest and least upset by this sad turn of events." A clerk, Otto Zinnie, recalled what happened when he and a matron from the camp drove the princess to her hearing at the federal courthouse in Philadelphia. "We were met by swarms of newsmen and photographers. She was smart as a whip when she defended herself in court. She sounded like a Supreme Court Judge. I never saw what made her so attractive. She was in her late forties then, and you wouldn't take a second look at her."[6]

Attractive or not, men found her irresistible. She had plenty of lovers over the years, and the next man to fall under her spell was Lemuel B. Schofield, director of the U.S. Immigration Service. The romance continued hot and heavy, and several months after her arrest, Schofield announced that he was releasing Princess Stephanie because she had promised to cooperate with the government and provide some very valuable information. She was later rearrested and spent the remainder of the war in Crystal City, Texas.

Logistics and other considerations dictated that German detainees from the Midwest be held in Chicago until they received their final internment orders. The women were separated from the men and taken to the Convent of the Good Shepherd on Grace Street on the city's north side. No more than a dozen women occupied the facility at any given time. The convent was a two-story building that covered most of a city block. Offices, classrooms, and a visiting room were situated on the first floor. The second floor contained a large hall with eighteen beds.

The sisters did their best to ensure that the women were comfortable and well taken care of during their stay. Since the convent didn't have a canteen, one of the sisters was assigned to shop in the local markets for any items their guests might need. The detainees were held at the convent until they were transferred to a permanent camp or allowed to join their husbands at the family camps in Texas.

Male prisoners were held at a converted three-story mansion complete with turrets and a rose garden. Located on South Ellis Avenue, it was surrounded on three sides by a six-foot wrought iron fence and a brick wall in the rear of the property. Even though armed guards patrolled the grounds and manned the guard post situated near the front door, security wasn't especially tight. With the changing of the guards, detainees assembled in a large hall on the main floor to be counted.

Six or seven bedrooms with their own bathrooms were located on the second floor off of a large open area that had once served as a dance floor. Each bedroom contained four steel army cots with thin mattresses, wool army blankets, and orange crates for nightstands. Beds had to be made up by breakfast time and detainees were only permitted to sit on the beds after lunch. The third floor originally served as the recreation area, but when the population of the facility became too large, it was transformed into a dormitory.

Detainees were counted in a daily bed check by the 11:00 p.m. shift change and again one hour later after lights out. If the count failed to match the previous shift's count, the guards would turn on the lights and do a recount. No one was allowed to go to sleep until everyone was accounted for.

The men were well treated during their stay on Ellis Avenue. They received good food and unlimited mail, and they had access to numerous books and magazines. Since there weren't a lot of activities to pass the time, they rotated the household chores such as scrubbing the floors, working in the kitchen, or tending a small outdoor garden. For security reasons, only those on the "garden detail" were allowed in the backyard.

Eberhard Fuhr described his experience when he and his brother arrived at the mansion in handcuffs. "We arrived late at night, and the other internees gave us a heartfelt welcome. We were there approximately three months. There were about twenty inmates. The number stayed fairly constant as internees were periodically sent to camps in North Dakota and Texas, occasionally released, or newly interned."[7]

In the spring and early summer of 1942, enemy alien males on Ellis Island who were considered potentially dangerous were loaded onto a sealed-off train with shuttered windows and transferred from INS control to the U.S. Army at Fort Meade, Maryland.

The Fort Meade welcoming committee made life miserable for those internees who had remained loyal to the United States and decided not to opt for a speedy repatriation to Germany. As far as the military was concerned, they were prisoners of war and covered by the Geneva Convention of 1929. The guards considered these men to be dangerous enemies, but in reality they were nothing more than butchers, bakers, shopkeepers, and mechanics, the ordinary people you would find in any city or town across America.

Internees were ordered to wear green government-issue khaki uniforms and live in four-man tents. Much to their dismay, they soon learned that their living quarters would flood after a heavy rain. The camp was surrounded by barbed wire, off limits signs, and machine guns. Armed guards patrolled the perimeter. FBI agents were present to keep tabs on suspected pro-Nazi ringleaders in the camp and to interrogate the prisoners, sometimes spiriting one or two of them off to unknown locations.[8]

Mail delivery was a big problem for the internees. Incoming mail was always months late. The postal censors in New York claimed that they were seriously understaffed and completely overwhelmed with the tremendous number of internee letters into and out of the camp.

One of the most serious problems facing the internees upon their arrival was the presence of captured German seamen already interned there. Transferred from Camp Upton, New York,[9] the seamen created a culture that was extremely pro-Nazi and nationalistic. They placed swastikas and pictures of Hitler in various buildings and living facilities and elected Hans Huttler, the ship's cook from the SS *Odenwald*, as their leader. The seamen organized mass gatherings and incited intimidation and violence to insure that their fellow inmates conformed to their ideology.

During the first months of confinement, the issue of repatriation literally tore the internee community apart. Those who chose not to be repatriated were considered traitors to the fatherland and were met with ridicule and violence. Given the conditions of their arrest and detention, it became a question of remaining loyal to the United States or accepting a speedy exchange and ending their confinement. Despite the bitterness that they must have felt, many of them elected not to accept repatriation.

Most of the internees were at Fort Meade for a relatively short time before they were ordered to pack their meager belongings and prepare to move on to other camps. In November 1942, six hundred prisoners were loaded onto trains and transferred to Camp Forrest, Tennessee.

Since its opening in May 1942, Camp Forrest received about

two hundred internees a month and was prepared for many more. When the contingent from Fort Meade arrived at the station, heavily armed soldiers met them to escort them to camp. The troops cordoned off the station, and when the men disembarked from the train, they were ordered to line up. Soldiers on trucks with mounted machine guns stood ready to open fire in case of trouble with these "dangerous enemies." They refused to believe the men were being detained simply because of their nationality and the misfortune of being in America at the outbreak of the war.

Immediately upon arrival at the camp, the internees were issued a set of regulations and instructions that were to be followed without question.[10]

1. When the National Anthem is played or "To the Colors" is sounded, internees will uncover, stand at attention, and face the music or colors.
2. An internee, if seated out of doors, will rise upon the approach of an officer, face toward him, and stand at attention. Internees actually at work will not cease work upon approach of the officer, unless the officer actually addresses him.
3. When an officer enters a room in which there are internees, the latter will stand at attention and uncover until the officer indicates otherwise or leaves the room.
4. An internee will stand at attention while addressing or being addressed by an officer.

Fortunately, the tensions over leadership between the pro-Nazis and anti-Nazi factions at Fort Meade did not follow the internees to their new home. The military authorities made it clear from the very beginning that the internees should elect their own spokesman by universal ballot. They believed that anyone selected by the camp population would be able to communicate the will and the wishes of the prisoners.

The internees selected Karl Mathey as leader and spokesman.[11] Not much is known about him, but he must have been a strong leader and able politician. He gained the confidence of the small but influential pro-Nazi group while still maintaining the support of the moderates in the camp. Under his leadership, the major frictions that flared up from time to time between the various groups were minimized.

Like any small community, there were the usual complaints of petty theft, hoarding of materials, excessive late night noises, lack of community housekeeping, and even the presence of a "peeping tom." The internees often administered their own brand of community discipline as illustrated in an article in the camp newspaper, *The Latrine*. In the case of one thief, the editor wrote, "A Mississippi hanging is too good for him."[12]

During the spring and winter of 1943, the internees found ways to pass the time. They played with a host of wild and domestic pets, tried their hands at arts and crafts, played soccer, and enrolled in courses ranging from physics to painting to foreign languages at the camp university. Commenting on the university, Joh Jung wrote:

> Some day you will leave this camp and be a free man again. People will no doubt ask you how you spent your time. It would be too bad if you simply vegetated, i.e., did little but eat and grow older. Imagine, on the other hand, their surprise, and your own satisfaction if you perfected yourself in your profession or learned a new one, studied and are mastering mathematics, a foreign language, physics, chemistry, shorthand, or some art.
>
> Now here is some advice you'll be thankful for: Come to our university. Here everything is free. Think of all the money you would have spent by taking lessons, visiting a school, college, or university in the outside world. Here everything is free. Professional men are happy to confer their knowledge, their skills to you without any charge. Their names and the subjects they are teaching follow in alphabetical order:

Achtner	B-19	physics, slide rule, geology
Austermann	A-9	mathematics
Biederbeck	A-4	mathematics
Dr. Culemann	B-19	English, physiology
Einor	B-11	shorthand
Guenther	B-2	drawing, painting
Jung	A-15	French, Italian, Spanish
Knetzing	B-14	drawing, painting
Laub	C-11	English

Dr. V. Yikusch	C-9	Chemistry
Plath	C-8	Spanish
Suppance	C-11	English
Wheeler-Hill	A-10	Russian
Willems	B-6	Electricity

New courses will be added from time to time. We intend to have some in geography, Greek, Latin, history, literature, and music. Come and see us. Let us know what subjects you are interested in. Watch this column for further announcements. Remember, here is your opportunity; don't fail to take advantage.[13]

When they were first interned, the prisoners were determined not to waste their time on useless activities. Since they couldn't practice their professions and trades, they set out to study, develop their hobbies, and keep physically fit. An article in the November 21, 1942, issue of *The Latrine* describes their efforts in starting their school.

The best example of what can be done is our school system, especially that of the new arrivals from Fort Meade. A few statistics will illustrate this point. During the month of October, more than 27% of the German internees at Meade felt the need for organized study so strongly that they attended ninety-two classes in thirty-eight subjects. Twenty-four teachers taught nearly five hundred students, and twenty special lectures were attended by a total of nine hundred men.

The fusion of the internees from the two areas at Meade and the men already at Camp Forrest has given a new and even stronger incentive to the school idea. More teachers are available; more students justify the introduction of new courses.

What we need is, of course, not an empty mess hall that could accommodate one class at a time, but four or five huts with enough room to conduct our more than 115 classes a week. We press our wish in the knowledge that the Geneva Convention calls for adequate facilities to further studies and schooling among internees at war.[14]

The Latrine was the major source of camp news for the internees. Because they were afraid that the prisoners might pass on sensitive information, the authorities required that it be printed in English.

With so many complaints from the internees that the paper should be printed in German, it became necessary for the editors to offer an explanation.

> An avalanche of indignation arose among our new comrades against the camp paper when we told them that this paper is written in the English language. May we ask you to hold on and let us explain before you condemn. It is our firm opinion that the language of our camp paper should be German. We are working toward this goal and are hopeful that we shall be able to give you a German camp paper in the near future. The reason for the use of English is that the authorities so far have not permitted any other language. However, at his recent visit to the camp, Dr. Fischer, head of the War Prisoner's Aid, promised to intervene in our behalf, and we expect action very soon.[15]

Month after month, rumors of breaking camp or transferring to a family camp came and went with the occasional news of a few lucky internees released on parole. When the announcement to break camp finally came in May 1943, the editors of *The Latrine* concluded,

> Our self-made organizations and institutions for sport and music, study and entertainment, including this voice of public opinions—purgative for ill humors—will and must definitely die with our departure from the oaks of Tennessee. Furniture and home decorations, flower gardens, the menagerie of reptiles, birds, and squirrels, together with our well-trained dogs and cats stay behind—bearing much testimony to endless hours of handicraft labors and fun. But more valuable than these self-made implements and toys, of which we shall soon be deprived, are those priceless possessions of idealism, our friendships and associations, our uplifting school and lecture, music and theater performances, and last but not least, the publication of our own news sheet.[16]

From Camp Forrest, married internees were reunited with wives and children at Seagoville or Crystal City, Texas, while single men were sent to Fort Lincoln, North Dakota, for the duration of the war.

Notes

1. Arnold Kramer, *Undue Process* (Lanham, Maryland: Rowman & Littlefield Publishers, 1997).
2. Lars Hemingstam, "*Drottingholm* and *Gripsholm*, The Exchange and Repatriation Voyages During WWII," www.salship.se/mercy.asp.
3. Author unknown, "Memories from the Dark Side," *Freedom of Information Times*.
4. Ibid.
5. Memo, State Department, *Princess Stefanie Von Hohenlohe Waldenburg*, October 28, 1941.
6. Ron Avery, "Ellis Island An Unwelcome Sight to Aliens," *Courier Post* (Camden, New Jersey, February 4, 1981).
7. Eberhard Fuhr, email to author, March 1, 2009.
8. John Heitman, May 10, 1998, *Enemies Are Human.* Paper presented to history department, University of Dayton, Dayton, Ohio.
9. Swiss Inspection Report to Secretary of War, *Concerning Conditions at Camp Upton POW Camp*, New York, April 3, 1942.
10. *Regulations for Information, Guidance, and Strict Compliance of All Persons Concerned*, Camp Forrest, Tennessee, May 23, 1942.
11. Alien Enemy Internment, Camp Forrest, Tennessee, RG 4, January 20, 1943.
12. Camp Forrest Newspaper, *The Latrine*, Vol. 2, No. 10, March 6, 1943.
13. Ibid., Vol. 1, No. 19, November 28, 1942.
14. Ibid., Vol. 1, No. 18, November 21, 1942.
15. Ibid., Vol. 1, No. 16, November 14, 1942.
16. Ibid., Vol. 2, No. 20, May 15, 1943.

SEVEN

THE SCHMITZ FAMILY

Recounted by John Schmitz

We have all read about the mass relocation of 120,000 Japanese from the West Coast shortly after Pearl Harbor to various camps in the interior, and ten thousand to internment camps. However, little is known about the selective internment of twelve thousand Germans and a number of Italians who were also considered dangerous enemy aliens. In an atmosphere of hostilities, fear, and racism, many were denied their basic constitutional rights, which is similar to our present situation regarding Muslims or people from the Middle East after 9/11.

One of the major reasons for the internment program was to have people available to exchange for American civilians interned by Japan and Germany. Many of our citizens worked and lived abroad and found themselves in internment camps. A good number of exchanges arranged by the American Red Cross took place during the war, involving thousands of internees.

My parents were not citizens, and Papa enjoyed listening to German music in our apartment in the Bronx. He also subscribed to a German magazine, and we were members of a German social club. All it took was a complaint from neighbors to the FBI that they thought he was a Nazi, and the hunt was on. Our apartment was searched and there were a number of interviews and then hearings with the result that Papa was branded a dangerous enemy alien. When asked if he would fight against Germany, he replied that he would rather fight against Japan. They said, "That is not the question." My father was thirty-five years old at the time, working as a waiter in a first-class restaurant, and married with three children ages eight, seven, and three, all born in New York City.

Processing and hearings took time, and while he was interned at Ellis Island, my mother took us on a train ride to Washington, DC, to see the president at the White House. Mama was going to tell FDR that her husband was not a Nazi and should be released. She was quite determined and had a lot of spunk. Needless to say, Mama didn't get to see the president but was advised to voluntarily join her husband.

We did that after storing our furniture with a good friend and neighbor. That's how we ended up interned on Ellis Island for three months before being shipped to Crystal City, Texas, in July 1943. We traveled with a group of other German families on a train ride lasting three days.

Crystal City was a small town about 110 miles southeast of San Antonio and close to the Mexican border. It was spinach country, and their claim to fame was the designation, "Spinach Capitol of the World." A large ten-foot statue of Popeye the Sailor stood in the town square. That was my first image of Crystal City. A migrant labor housing facility had been converted to an internment camp. Ten-foot barbed wire fences were erected, with high towers for armed guards in each corner and at the center of the perimeter fence. Over five hundred additional units were constructed to house the detainees, as well as schools, a hospital, maintenance facilities, mess halls, a post office, and other buildings to make it a self-contained city patrolled by INS guards.

About two hundred acres comprised the camp itself. Detainees under guard worked an additional three hundred acres of surrounding farmland outside the fence. Every man in the camp had a job and was required to work, for which he was paid ten cents an hour. Special plastic coins of various denominations were the currency used in the camp, rationed according to the size of each family. Ice and milk were delivered daily to both loosely divided sections of the camp by German and Japanese rotating crews. Meals were prepared in separate mess halls for those German and Japanese aliens not living in units having kitchens, and they were in the majority.

The camp housed butchers, bakers, barbers, clerks, and teachers—English, German, and Japanese for the three schools in the camp—as well as internee nurses and doctors. Parents determined which school or two schools their children would attend. Classes were generally held in the morning because of the heat. A volunteer fire department with one truck staffed by internees provided security for this hazard. A U.S. public health officer and head nurse ran the hospital. Five detainee nurses, two of whom were Japanese women, also staffed it. Detainee nurse's aides were also trained and served well.

More than 250 babies were born in this hospital, all U.S. citizens. However, their birth certificates read from the Texas Department of Health, Zavala County, Precinct #3, Alien Internment Camp, Crystal City, Texas. My sister Christa was born in the hospital on September 23, 1944, so we would later be released as a family of six. In March 1945, I had a double hernia operation due to playground mishaps. Medical and dental treatments were obviously free of charge and very good.

A large irrigation tank used to provide water to adjacent farms had a seepage problem and turned the area into a swamp. A one-hundred-yard diameter swimming pool was constructed at this site at a cost of $2,500 for materials. The detainees provided labor, and the pool became the main recreation activity for most of the year. It was completed in late 1943 and staffed by qualified detainee lifeguards. This was where my sister and I learned to swim and soon passed the test to be permitted in the twelve-foot-deep end with two diving boards. For us kids, as well as most parents, the pool was the best thing since sliced bread. Water was pumped into the pool daily and discharged to irrigate the adjacent farms.

Recreation for adults and teenagers was available through sports. Teams and leagues were formed for softball, basketball, soccer, Ping-Pong, tennis, judo, and others. The Germans would play the Japanese in all sports, and those games drew the most spectators. Separate Japanese and German recreation areas showed outdoor movies once a week, but we had to bring our own chairs from home. There was also a café serving snacks, sodas, and beer, which were rationed. The adults were periodically issued ration coupons for cigarettes and beer. Our father worked at the café for ten cents an hour.

There were about sixteen hundred minor children in the camp at one time, with a total detainee population of thirty-six hundred. It was a huge playpen for us kids. There was very little vehicular traffic, so parents didn't have to worry about their children being run over. No fear of getting lost, thanks to the fence.

The most popular song in both areas of the camp was "Don't Fence Me In." Language was not a problem since we could all fall back on English. We did not play war games, instinctively realizing not to go there. Instead, we played "cowboys and Indians," which was a safer alternative taken from the western movies we watched.

My father initially wanted to be repatriated to Germany after being interned, to be exchanged in one of the trades for Americans in Germany. Fortunately, we were never put on the earlier list, and Mama, after removing us from the list, convinced Papa that it would be foolish to return to a defeated war-torn country. Sanity prevailed, and Papa removed himself from the list.

In July 1946, three years after our arrival, we were released from internment in Crystal City and driven to the train in San Antonio for our trip back to New York City. We were warned not to talk about our internment experience to anyone. We returned to life in New York as though it had never happened and tried to resume a normal existence.

A welfare agency representative, probably set up by INS, met us upon our arrival and found us hotel accommodations in down-town Manhattan just a few blocks from the Empire State Building. I thought it was great riding the elevators up and down and having the elevator operator say "hi" and "bye" to us. Do you remember the operators expertly bringing the car to a perfect stop on the floor using their power slide controller? This was before automated push buttons put them out of a job.

I stayed with Tante Elsa Scholz, my mother's girlfriend from her hometown in Germany, Leobschuetz, in Schesier. She and her husband were superintendents of a six-story apartment building off 200th Street and Webster Avenue in the Bronx. That arrangement got me out of the cramped quarters of the hotel in Manhattan. I had a great time and was always playing baseball in the summer with the neighborhood kids in the park only a block away. The kids even called me "Scholzie," thinking I was Tante Elsa's son Donald, who was about eight years older than me. He did let me use his baseball glove, warning me not to lose it.

Papa had to find a job as well as an apartment since it was very crowded in those two hotel rooms. The war was over, and the returning troops were starting their own families in their own apartments. Demand greatly exceeded supply, but we were able to get a five-room apartment laid out "railroad flat" style in a six-family apartment house. Oh yes, there was one bathroom—just a toilet in the hall between the two apartments on each floor. To get this apartment, we had to become the "supers," cleaning and caring for the building, collecting the monthly rent from tenants (we lived rent free), and keeping the coal furnace going to supply hot water and steam heat in winter. My father found a good job as a waiter in Luechows Restaurant on 14th Street while contemplating what the INS was going to do.

My parents tried the political route by "contributing" $1,000 in 1948 to a politician to sponsor a private bill for the 81st Congress, Senate Bill S.658, "A Bill for the Relief of Adolph Max Schmitz" to cancel the outstanding warrant of deportation. The bill considered him to have been lawfully admitted to the U.S. on September 18, 1928.

Papa surprised us with the fact that he had saved enough money for a down payment on a townhouse in the upper Bronx. We moved uptown in January 1949 from 154th Street in the lower Bronx to 238th Street off White Plains Road.

Mama found time to write to the president concerning the deportation of Papa. The INS responded. They noted the private bill S.658 was in the works in the current Congress and chose not to act pending resolution of the bill.

I guess the INS lost interest in Papa or his case just fell through the cracks for a while. We wanted Papa to gain legal entry to the U.S. We children went about our business, which was to get an education. Louise and I graduated from high school, Bill and Christa were enrolled in elementary school, and life went on. The New York

Protestant Episcopal City Mission Society had taken our case almost from the day we got off the train from Crystal City and was still trying to prevent Papa's deportation.

After becoming a U.S. citizen in the early fifties, Mama sailed for Germany with Louise, Bill, and Christa for a very long vacation on the Holland America lines. Papa and I stayed home to work. He continued as a waiter while I ran Mama's candy store and luncheonette by myself. I had planned to attend Concordia Jr. College in Bronxville, New York, and was promised the profits for the summer after all the bills were paid. Great experience, that slave labor working for the family!

The wheels of the INS and the Department of Justice were turning, and we received a letter dated 13 June 1956, advising Papa he could get an immigrant visa to enter the U.S. A following letter of 16 July scheduled Papa for an interview for reexamination for his immigrant visa. Papa was to appear at the U.S. Consulate in Montreal, Canada, on 13 September 1957, the result being that Mama, Papa, and my brother Bill took a very long car ride from New York City to Canada. Papa was able to enter the U.S. as a legal immigrant, almost thirty years from the time he first set foot on American soil. Some officials asked Papa if he was going to apply for citizenship papers, and his polite reply was that he really didn't need them now.

EIGHT

CAMP SEAGOVILLE, TEXAS

Detainees arrested west of the Mississippi were generally sent to Camp Seagoville until they could be transferred to other camps. Located southeast of Dallas, it was originally designed as a minimum-security reformatory for female inmates. In 1942, it was taken over by the INS and converted into an internment facility for Germans, Italians, Japanese, and Latin Americans. Seagoville was initially intended as a camp for families in which both parents had been interned while they waited for repatriation or transfer to the main family camp at Crystal City, Texas.[1] Toward the end of the war, Seagoville became a women-only camp, although some children were held there with their mothers.

Camp Seagoville covered 830 acres, much of it farmland and pasture. In the latter part of their internment, prisoners could use a small wooded section for picnics and other outings. Spacious mani-cured lawns fronted the compound of twelve limestone-trimmed, colonial-style, red brick buildings. Arranged in a quadrangle and connected by paved walkways, facilities consisted of dormitories, a recreation building, a beauty shop, a barbershop, a storehouse, a power plant, a maintenance shop, and a fully equipped hospital staffed and operated by the United States Public Health Service.[2]

The internee living quarters were divided into two parts. One part included six two-story brick buildings facing the quadrangle, each containing from forty to seventy-five single sleeping rooms in addition to dining rooms, recreation rooms, and a kitchen. As the population of the camp increased, the government constructed sixty prefabricated, temporary, sixteen-by-sixteen-foot wooden "victory huts." These buildings and a mess hall made up what became known as *the colony.*

Families occupied some of the huts, while one or two people occupied others. Internees in each house organized their own kitchens and prepared and served foodstuffs delivered from the main warehouse. The camp dietician was required to adapt the daily menus to reflect the ethnic values of the internees. The Japanese ate foods that were unfamiliar to the Germans and vice versa. As long as the total daily rations of proteins and carbohydrates met the specific guidelines of the Geneva Convention, requests for specific food items were usually honored.

Camp superintendent, Dr. Amy Stannard, remembered one of the first Thanksgivings the internees shared. "We found that they didn't want the traditional American turkey for Thanksgiving. So they had other things: the Germans wanted roast beef and whatnot and the Japanese wanted cherry pie. We incorporated it into their menu for the day."[3]

Built to look like a college campus, the resemblance ended ten feet from the chain-link fence topped with barbed wire that surrounded the camp. A solid white line down the middle of the road encircled the camp and marked the boundary that the internees could not cross. The gatehouse at the entrance to the camp was manned at all times by unarmed Border Patrol agents. They patrolled the enclave on foot and on horseback and were under strict orders not to enter the internees' quarters except on special orders or in an emergency.

Camp Seagoville may have been the most civilized camp in the INS internment system, but to the internees it was still a prison. To quote an old Spanish saying, "It doesn't matter that the cage is golden, it is still a cage."[4]

Many mothers suffered the anguish of long separations from their husbands and children. Pregnant women gave birth upon their arrival at camp, while others suffered miscarriages from the stress of internment. In addition to the female prisoners, married couples with children, German and Japanese diplomats and their families, and other internees from Latin America were also held at the camp.

In his article, "Jewish Internees in the American South, 1942–1945," Harvey Strum wrote that there were a total of eighty-one Jews among the Germans from Latin America. Most Latin American countries didn't really target the Jews for deportation, but if they happened to arrest them, they didn't bother to release them. On the other hand, the anti-Semitic governments of British Honduras and Panama were happy to include them in their roundups.[5]

Those Jews who escaped from the horrors of Nazi Germany or appeared to be involved in suspicious activities were sent to the Balboa Detention Center in the Canal Zone. After weeks of intensive interrogation by the U.S. Army, they were permitted to rejoin their families and the other Jews who had been dispersed to Seagoville and other camps in Georgia and Florida.

In late February 1943, thanks to the efforts of numerous Jewish and Catholic organizations, the American Civil Liberties Union, and influential members of the State Department, the majority of Jews were paroled and allowed to resettle wherever they could find sponsors. Some of the Jews had their status changed when they joined the military, but the rest were subject to deportation at the end of the war.

By November 1943, the Justice Department decided that the Jews no longer posed a threat to the United States. Parole supervision was lifted, and internees were released on a case-by-case basis. It wasn't until 1946 that the last Jewish prisoners were released. Two of the Jews voluntarily returned to their homes in South America, but four died while in captivity. Seventy-five of them chose to live and work in the United States.

The first detainees to arrive at the camp were women and children from Latin America. They had previously been incarcerated in the Panama Canal Zone, and when brought to the United States, they were held at the immigration station in New Orleans. Exhausted from the long train ride, they arrived at camp late in the day. The administration prepared a hot meal that was served at long tables in the hospital's quarantine section. In her daily report, Dr. Stannard wrote, "It was pathetic to see how frightened they were and so hungry. They ate ravenously, and at the same time snatching food to hide inside their clothing, as though they expected to be starved later on."[6]

The women were uneducated and confused and few of them spoke English. Fortunately, some of the staff spoke Spanish and were able to act as interpreters along with two young female internees. Staff members of German and Italian descent translated for the Germans and Italians in the group. One woman who understood the culture and language of the Japanese served as a liaison between the Japanese prisoners and the American administration.

In late 1942, as described by Dr. Stannard, the husbands arrived and joined their families.

> On the following day after their arrival, a small delegation of German men came to the hospital. After brief introductions, they were invited to visit their sick children. The fathers insisted upon removing the children immediately to the family quarters. None of the children were critically ill, but in need of bed rest and nursing care.
>
> The men ignored the questioning as to whether the mothers wanted this relocation and indicated that they would take the responsibility of caring for the children. The response was accepted without arguing. In a day or so, the sickest children were returned to the hospital. Raw potato poultices and home remedies had not cured boils and other illnesses.[7]

To overcome the boredom of camp life, the internees did whatever they could to pass the time. The men kept busy with maintenance work and administrative jobs. The women organized plays, outdoor open-air concerts, theatrical performances, and songfest. They also maintained the camp library with its three thousand books in German, Spanish, English, and Japanese donated by the YMCA and the German government.

There were educational opportunities available for those who chose to take advantage of them. Since many of the internees were proficient in various trades and professions, they taught classes in everything from German, Italian, Spanish, and English, to stenography and decorative woodworking. Two of the most popular areas for the women were the weaving room and a modestly equipped garment factory. Prisoners learned to sew drapes and weave rugs, and if they desired, they could learn, teach, or engage in the dressmaking trade.

The first commander of the camp was an affable Irishman, Joseph O'Rourke. Like most Irishmen, he loved the children and they loved him. Perhaps because of the large staff he had to work with or because he got tired of the many complaints from his German charges, he had his moments of irritation. Every once in a while O'Rourke lost his temper and cussed out one of his subordinates. He was a social drinker, but never drank while on duty.

On more than one occasion, O'Rourke had to deal with Princess Stephanie Hohenlohe. She arrived at the hospital on a stretcher and was placed in a single room that had been prepared for her. The staff had been advised that she was extremely ill, but after a careful examination, the doctors reported that they couldn't find anything wrong with her. Two days later she asked to be released to the German internee group. Her fellow inmates weren't happy to see her.

A few days later, the Princess returned to the hospital. She requested sleeping pills, but the doctors refused. She complained to O'Rourke, who in turn called the medical officer to insist that her request be granted. When the doctor again refused, O'Rourke went to town and bought the sleeping pills. He paid for them out of his own pocket.

O'Rourke was replaced by his assistant, Dr. Amy Stannard, a government psychiatrist and the only female warden in the INS prison system. Thanks to her psychiatric skills, she was able to deal with the numerous complaints and demands of the spokesmen for the Germans, Franz Wirz, Hans Ackerman, and Franz Stangl.

In the early months of confinement, complaints were usually centered on food. The Germans wanted more chicken than the camp budget allowed and demanded fresh fruits and vegetables that weren't available in the local market. When the internees asked for an increase in the daily milk ration, Dr. Stannard raised it from one pint per person per day to one quart per day for children up to age eighteen, pregnant and nursing mothers, and those on special diets.

As time went by, the complaints became more vocal. The internees were dissatisfied with the movie schedules, visiting speakers, censorship of their mail, and the requirement that they inform the camp administration of parties in their quarters where beer was to be served. In fact, the Germans seemed to complain about everything, and they didn't care who knew it. Being a good psychiatrist and an excellent administrator, Dr. Stannard listened to their complaints and tried to do everything she could to alleviate their concerns.

There were occasional problems that neither Dr. Stannard nor the internees could resolve no matter how hard they tried. One such problem occurred just before the end of the war in Europe, and many former internees remember it with anger to this day. In late April 1945, the War Department issued a directive reducing the prisoners' daily ration.

The directive stated, "Due to the nation-wide shortage of food supplies, ration allowances are to be revised, effective immediately. Fresh meat, eggs, milk and milk products, fats, fresh fruits, and coffee are to be sharply reduced." As a result of the directive, the menu changed to spaghetti, macaroni, cereal, vegetables, fatty meat, and boiled cabbage.

Why the War Department issued the declaration was never made clear. One theory that circulated around the camp was that vast amounts of food were required for the large number of American troops fighting in Europe and the Pacific. Another theory was that so many boys were drafted into the military that there was a shortage of field hands to work the farms.

Just as in other camps, friction between the pro-Nazis and the anti-Nazis was commonplace. Strange as it may seem, the Nazis had more influence with the camp administration than the anti-Nazis. Friends of the Nazi spokesmen doled out whatever jobs were available. The pro-Nazis and the Bundists got the best jobs, but those who refused to subscribe to their beliefs had to take what was left. The Nazis considered the anti-Nazis to be traitors. They started a whisper campaign accusing them of being FBI informants. The Nazis also excluded anti-Nazis from certain areas of the camp and tampered with their food.

Internees received three dollars a month in scrip to buy the bare necessities from the camp store. It was more then adequate to purchase their daily needs until March 23, 1943 when the Treasury Department announced that the 1941 law freezing all Axis assets also applied to the internees. Internees were then required to complete a two-page form listing all of their assets. Most prisoners had already turned control of their assets over to someone who wasn't an enemy alien, only to see their homes, businesses, and bank accounts disappear in bankruptcies and outright theft.

New internees continued to arrive at Camp Seagoville until June 1945 when it was closed as an "enemy alien" internment camp. Prisoners were transferred to other camps or returned to Germany.

NOTES

1. *Camp Seagoville*, German American Internee Coalition.
2. World War II Internment Camps, *Handbook of Texas Online*, www.tshaonline.org/handbook/online/articles/WW/quwby.html.
3. Interview with Dr. Stannard, Japanese American World War II Evaluation Oral History Project: Part B, University of California, November 30, 1978.
4. Richard Santos, Chairman, Zavala County Historical Commission.
5. Harvey Strum, "Jewish Internees in the American South, 1942–1945," *American Jewish Archives*, Spring 1990, No. 1, p. 27.
6. Interview with Dr. Stannard, Japanese American World War II Evaluation Oral History Project: Part B, University of California, November 30, 1978.
7. Ibid.

NINE

PERUVIANS REMEMBER
U.S. CONCENTRATION CAMPS

Recounted by Daniel Goya, translated by Cathy Cockrell

B orn on September 6, 1930, Augusto Kague Castillo was only eleven years old on the day the police detained his father. They lived in Jauja, Junin, where his family owned a restaurant. One morning, young Augusto went out to buy rice for Mantaro Kague, his father, and never saw him again. For three months they received no news of Mantaro. His loved ones assumed the worst, until a letter arrived. In the letter, Kague told how he had been taken out of the country and locked in a prison in the United States. The letter was so covered with stains that they were unable to read some of the words and even entire sentences.

"It was censored," Augusto said. "We answered my father's letters and for two years we received his answers censored. During his absence, my father's business went bankrupt. There was no one to run it, and we soon began to live in misery. They threw us out of our house because we couldn't pay the rent, and we began to wander like gypsies, staying in the houses of friends and family members." Theirs was one of almost a thousand families that the government of Manuel Prado Ugarteche surrendered to the United States after the bombing of Pearl Harbor on December 7, 1941.

Everyone was detained in a concentration camp near Crystal City, in the burning desert of the state of Texas. The Peruvians were part of twenty-two hundred Japanese and Nisei deported by thirteen

Latin American countries allied with North America. Those whose fathers and mothers were detained and forcibly sent to the North American internment center, solely because they were born in Japan or were the children of Japanese immigrants, became desperate, and the community in Peru had to look for ways for fathers and sons to meet again.

For the Kagues, there was an element of luck. The wife of Enrique Kague, Micaela, met a friend whose husband was also in Crystal City. The friend said that her husband wanted her to join him in the camp, but that she didn't want to because of their children. The friend offered that Micaela should travel in her place, and that's what she did. Soon afterward, she left for Texas from the port of Talara.

"It was a twenty-day trip," remembered Augusto, whose mother's family lived in Piura. "The men traveled in the lower deck of the boat, and the women and children above deck. Each week, they would let the men come up for fifteen or twenty minutes to walk and smoke a little. Some of them put three cigarettes in their mouths at the same time and smoked. When we arrived in New Orleans, the U.S. officials asked us to remove our clothes. We thought they were going to kill us right there, but they sprayed us with insecticides and soap. They received us as if we were infected animals."

Before the mass deportation, anti-Japanese sentiment was evident in various levels of society. President Prado didn't hide his antipathy for the children of the Land of the Rising Son, and the Aprista Party, through its official mouthpiece, *La Tribuna*, leaked rumors of supposed plots by Japanese residents to take over the country.

On May 13, 1940, two years before the deportations began, a riot by a mob of students from the Guadalupe Academy led to the destruction of six hundred Japanese-owned businesses and killed ten citizens of the same origin. In an official visit to Washington in May 1942, Prado had a meeting with President Franklin D. Roosevelt and General George C. Marshall in which they requested his collusion in the deportation of 17,500 Japanese, regardless of whether they had been born in Peru or had Peruvian citizenship. Roosevelt and Marshall considered them potentially dangerous enemies. Prado accepted this and lost no time in satisfying his hosts.

The same day as the attack on Pearl Harbor, German Yaki Hishii had just turned ten and was walking with his father, Sentei, and his mother, Ichi, on the streets of Lima. Suddenly they realized that something was wrong. People looked at them strangely. Coincidentally, on block after block, people turned to stare at them, some with suspicion and others with fear. When they got back to the house, they heard on the radio that Japan had attacked Pearl Harbor.

Two months later, German Yaki was playing in the street when he saw a truck pass with many Japanese inside it. One of them hurled out a rolled-up piece of paper. Yaki opened it. The words were written in Japanese. Yaki took the paper to his father, Sentei Yaki, who recognized it as a farewell message from one of the detainees who had been unable to speak with his family. Sentei, accordingly, brought the letter to the loved ones of the deported man. From that day, Yaki slept uneasily, believing that one day, the authorities would come rapping and take his father away.

A few years later, the nightmare came to pass. Uniformed men came looking for Yaki's father in his home on the 12th of January 1943. They took him away without explanation, although Sentei Yaki already guessed what awaited him. Six months of anguish and uncertainty later, German Yaki and his mother received a letter in which they were granted permission to live at Crystal City internment camp.

The Yaki family was part of the 17,500 Japanese that President Roosevelt and his friend, Prado, wanted to keep in detention at whatever cost. They created the blacklist jointly. The definitive version of the list came out September 13, 1944, under the title "Official List of Unwelcome Foreigners." For his part, Roosevelt wanted more prisoners of Japanese origin to exchange for U.S. prisoners of war.

"Life in Crystal City was a life without liberty. The center was surrounded by barbed wire, preventing any possibility of escape. Cowboys with rifles and horses appeared each hour patrolling the area to prevent escapes," recalls German Yaki. "All of the houses were prefabricated. The foreign detainees lived in these small wooden buildings. Besides us there were Germans."

Bathrooms were communal, and each family had to take turns using the toilets. On the south edge of Crystal City, there was a hospital, and on the northwest, a baseball field. The prefabricated housing was on the east side. On the southeast was a preschool in which children were taught to speak English. The detainees were responsible for the upkeep of the camp. Everyone earned the same amount, ten cents an hour, which came to less than a dollar a day.

German Yaki indicated that in Crystal City there was only one form of currency, the only form the detainees could use. Some of it carried inscriptions as to what one was allowed to buy so that the detainees wouldn't try to buy something that was prohibited by their U.S. wardens. "We weren't allowed to exercise choice about anything," German Yaki said with sadness.

One morning, the fire alarm sounded. The detainees thought that a house was on fire, but quickly realized what was happening. In English and Japanese, it was announced over the loudspeaker that Japan had lost the war and surrendered. The date was September 2, 1945. Some received the news with relief, imagining their speedy release. Others refused to believe that Japan had been defeated, and took the news as a lie told by North Americans.

According to the Nisei for Civil Rights and Redress, of the 2,264 prisoners in the camp, 945 Japanese from Peru were deported to a decimated Japan once the war ended. Another 300 remained in the United States as illegals and fought to obtain citizenship, while 100 returned to Peru.

TEN

CAMP CRYSTAL CITY, TEXAS

Located about 40 miles south of Uvalde, Texas, near the Nueces River, and 120 miles southwest of San Antonio, the Crystal City camp for families was the largest internment facility in the INS system. The town was created in the early 1900s when developers Carl Groos and E. J. Buckingham purchased a ten-thousand-acre ranch and sold it off in small parcels. Since the surrounding area was home to vast vegetable farms, they also constructed a massive labor camp to house the thousands of migratory workers needed to work in the fields.[1]

Sometime in the 1930s, the camp was taken over by the Farm Security Administration, but was reassigned to the INS in late 1942 for the express purpose of converting it into a family internment camp. Situated on 240 acres of land, the camp already contained 41 three-room cottages, 118 one-room shelters, numerous service buildings, and an adequate utility service to accommodate a population of two thousand.[2]

Camp Crystal City was originally intended as a relocation camp for two thousand Japanese detainees and their families. The first Germans to arrive in camp were brought as manual labor to expand existing facilities in preparation for the Japanese internees who were scheduled to arrive in a few months. The plan was for the Germans to construct additional buildings to house the new arrivals and then move them on to other camps.

The Germans protested this arrangement and refused to work unless they were allowed to live in the completed buildings. After lengthy negotiations, the INS accepted their demands. Since the Geneva Convention required separate accommodations for each nationality, the Germans and the Japanese were housed in segregated sections of the camp.

With the arrival of the first group of Japanese, it soon became apparent that the camp would have to be expanded to accommodate in excess of 3,500 people. This required increasing the size of the internment area, moving the fence several hundred yards from its initial location, and constructing hundreds of buildings and facilities wherever space could be found. Many of the early internees were required to help with the new construction.

By July 1, 1945, the camp consisted of 694 buildings, of which the INS, at a cost of over one million dollars, constructed 519. By the end of the war, camp staffing had reached the authorized strength of 161 personnel. This included administrators, INS guards, supply clerks, medical personnel, maintenance crews, and educators. An additional 200 craftsmen and laborers were employed for various jobs in and around the camp. As camp administrator, Joseph O'Rourke supervised the day-to-day operations. He served as camp commander for much of the war.[3]

The first internees arrived on December 12, 1942. It was decided to temporarily house thirty-five German families from Ellis Island and Camp Forrest, Tennessee, until adequate facilities were ready for them at Seagoville. Because their stay was intended to be temporary, the staff roped off twenty-nine of the three-room cottages for the use of the internees. Border Patrol agents were brought in to provide surveillance for the internees because the compound fence was still under construction and there weren't enough guards.

The next group of internees arrived on February 2, 1943, with twelve German males from the Kenedy, Texas, Internment Camp and 131 Germans from Costa Rica. On February 13, 1943, one additional German male was transferred from Kenedy, and the Corrigan party of 93 Germans from Ellis Island arrived February 19, 1943. The first group from the Seagoville Internment Camp was received March 10, 1943, and consisted of 1 German male, 4 females, and 2 children, and our first Japanese consisting of 14 women and 14 children. The first camp birth occurred on March 10, a German male. On March 17, 1943, two more groups were received: 23 Japanese males from Camp Livingston, Louisiana, and 4 German males from Stringtown, Oklahoma. On March 23, 1943, 94 Japanese males were brought in from Lordsburg, New Mexico, having been transferred to Crystal City in advance of their families for the purpose of assisting with the construction and incidental work preparatory to completion of quarters for family occupancy. The arrival of this group brought our camp population to 523: 378 Germans and 145 Japanese.[4]

Six different types of living quarters were available to the internees: from twelve-by-sixteen-foot one-room shelters for childless couples and couples with an infant or small child, to buildings consisting of four small apartments without indoor plumbing, to three-room cottages containing five hundred square feet of floor space and indoor toilets and baths. Tarpaper victory huts were later constructed to accommodate the mass influx of prisoners from other camps.

The cottages were designed for larger families and those suffering from illness or claiming special circumstances. Most families added extra rooms and built porches with lumber taken from the supply yards. Everyone tried to beautify their homes by planting flower gardens from seeds ordered from Montgomery Ward catalogs. They also planted vegetable gardens to supplement their daily diets. Meals were eaten family style at home or cafeteria style in a common mess hall.

Since there were no toilets and baths in the apartments or victory huts, internees were required to use central bath and latrine facilities. With the exception of the huts, each housing unit was equipped with a stove, a kitchen sink, and running water. The government supplied an initial allowance of cooking utensils, furniture, bedding, and an icebox. When an item became worn out and no longer usable, internees were required to turn it in to the Internal Relations Division before a replacement item would be issued.

The winter of 1942–43 was the coldest on record for south Texas. When it rained, mud was everywhere. When it snowed, icicles hung from the eves. Subsequent winters weren't quite as cold, though there was the occasional snowfall.

Interned from July 1943 to April 1947, two years after the war ended, Eberhard Fuhr remembers the living quarters at Crystal City. "Heat was via a round kerosene stove a foot in diameter and about two feet tall. The kitchen stove was a two-burner kerosene stove. The icebox was an ice box where cooling was via cakes of ice delivered daily. There was no running water in the quadriplexes. Bathing and the necessities were performed in a centralized bathhouse, unheated as I recall. There was one bathhouse for twenty units."[5]

Internees received a subsistence allowance that could be used to purchase food items from a central grocery and meat market operated on the basis of a general store. The money was in the form of tokens that resembled chips used in gambling casinos. The tokens were exchanged for food commodities at a stipulated price. Each day, teams of internees took turns delivering the twenty-five hundred quarts of milk required by the sixteen hundred children living in the camp. Other internees delivered the daily ration of blocks of ice for the iceboxes in each house. The ice was especially important to keep food and milk cold in the summer when temperatures reached 120 degrees Fahrenheit.

One of the major activities for the women was shopping. Every morning, hundreds of housewives left their quarters for a morning shopping tour. Long lines of women pushed their homemade shopping carts down the street and parked them in front of the store. When finished shopping for their daily needs, the women loaded the groceries into the carts and headed home.

In the early years, the distribution of clothing was a major problem for both the administration and the internees. A portion of a supply building was set aside as a distribution point, and all clothing was received and issued by a group of German and Japanese internees under the supervision of the chief supply officer. The first stocks consisted of work clothes for the men. It wasn't until later that clothes were available for the women and children.

To prevent friction between the internee groups and to simplify procedures, the supply officer instituted a card system for each person listing minimum needs, size, etc. An internee clerk would go to the shelf, select the proper size (or close to it), and put the articles in a paper bag. Internees had to take what was available and more often than not, the sizes were incorrect.

Because there were so many problems with this system and because the internees lodged so many complaints, a new system of distribution was developed. A large building with counters, shelving, and a cash register was constructed to meet the needs of the prisoners. The merchandise from the old store was sorted and placed on the shelves of the new location, and on May 17, 1944, it opened for business.

With some minor differences, the new store resembled a dry goods store in any small city in America. Dress racks and shelves were filled with merchandise that had arrived a few days before. The women lined up for hours and when the doors opened, they ran in screaming and shoving each other out of the way in a rush to get to the dress racks. It was all the staff could do to maintain order as the women fought to get the dress of their choice. This was the first time since they were interned that the prisoners were allowed to select something they really wanted.

Since the end of the war, some internees may have forgotten specific details of their time in Crystal City or may have chosen not to talk about it. But one thing they all could agree on was the hot Texas summers.

From June to September, the temperatures hovered around 120 degrees Fahrenheit. Sunburns and heat rashes were common, and the prisoners also had to deal with dust devils, sand storms, scorpions, red ants, rattlesnakes, mosquitoes, insects, and other animal life they'd never encountered before.

Living quarters were stifling due to a lack of any type of cooling, and many of the occupants suffered from heat stroke. A strange comment by an official of the Medical Division that "the houses are too hot, and it is to the Medical Division's interest that they are insulated or air conditioned to avoid having to treat a few individuals for heat stroke" brought some interesting responses from former internees.

John A. Schmitz, who describes himself as an internee alumnus of the class of July '43 to July '46, said, "Yes, we definitely DID NOT have air conditioning units in the private bungalows, and I know for certain the multifamily units did NOT have AC. The only comfort we had was the 10 p.m. breeze that blew in from the Gulf Coast most evenings. Since I was a ten-year-old lad, I can only recall what happened in my circle of friends. Crystal City was mostly HOT, HOT, HOT."[6]

Gunther Graber stated, "There was another level of air conditioning, a sandstorm that deposited about 1 or two inches of fine dust inside the bungalow in spite of closed doors and windows. I am also sure that 'creature comforts' were not on the top of the list for the internees, Germans or Japanese."[7]

The one place the internees could cool off from the excessive heat of the day was the camp swimming pool. Before the pool could be dug, it was necessary to clean out an irrigation canal in a swampy area near the fence, entirely overgrown with water hyacinths. Fed by artesian wells, the canal carried water to vegetable gardens and citrus groves inside the camp, and to farms outside the fence. Once the internees arrived on the premises, the canal was deemed too small for its intended purpose.

In order to make the canal usable for storage of water or any other purpose, the administration conscripted revolving labor teams made up of Germans and Japanese to clean out the hyacinths and enlarge the area for a reservoir. The internees received no pay, but in return for their labor, the camp administration permitted them to use the reservoir as a swimming pool. After it had been worked on for several days, they lined the pool with concrete, the only contribution the authorities made to the project.

An Italian internee from Honduras designed the reservoir. He was a civil engineer and had worked on similar projects in his own country before his arrest. In conjunction with interned German civil engineers, they incorporated the swimming pool into the irrigation system.

The pool was a large circular structure approximately 150 feet in diameter. It had both a shallow and a deep end, a platform in the middle, and a diving board that was in constant use throughout the day. Lifeguards were paid ten cents an hour to provide protection for the swimmers. Despite the lifeguards and almost wall-to-wall people in the pool, two young Japanese girls died from drowning on the hottest day of summer.[8]

Like children everywhere, swimming was the favorite activity.

Art Jacobs had a special fondness for the pool and spent most of his free time there. "Each morning about seven, I would head for the pool, and usually I was the first one there. During daylight hours, when I was not in school, I practically lived in the swimming pool. We dove, we swam, and just played, but each tried to be more macho than the next guy with the diving."[9]

In addition to the swimming pool, the internees had access to numerous recreational and entertainment programs. These activities included soccer, baseball, tennis, basketball, volleyball, and indoor parties and games. Tennis courts, baseball diamonds, soccer fields, and volleyball courts were scattered around the camp wherever vacant spaces could be found.

The children of the internees found a lot of ways to keep busy. John A. Schmitz remembered one of his favorite pastimes.

> John A. Schmitz here, who definitely remembers knocking my sister Louise off her stilts and into the mud and muck after a good rain. Maybe she knocked me off too, but, of course, I would have erased that from my memory—save the victories and forget the defeats. The hardest part was learning how to DO IT. We first started to get on by leaning on the wall of a building, probably the latrines (bathrooms and washrooms) since they were more centrally located. Then one mastered the art of walking. Getting off, of course, was not a problem (gravity). Learning how to step/ jump on without falling off took some practice. Uebung macht der Meister=practice makes perfect. You could also run pretty fast on stilts—good escape tactic.[10]

Eberhard Fuhr found that when it came to the rainy season, the stilts weren't only for games. "When those heavy rains came, the ditches filled up in a hurry and could run fairly swiftly. The stilts would come in handy crossing any street. That too, was the biggest problem in getting to the latrines when those heavy rainstorms hit and those foot-deep ditches had to be crossed."[11]

Most internees believed it was important to honor their cultural heritage. They presented recitals, dramas, musicals, and related cultural activities, and enthusiastically celebrated numerous holidays. For the Germans, the major festive day was May Day, followed by Christmas and Easter.

Art Jacobs remembered seeing a Maypole during his early days of internment. "When we were inside the camp, I noticed that there was a large pole with streamers of many colors hanging from the pole. I asked my father about the significance of the pole and its streamers. He replied, 'That's a Maypole, and it is part of a May Day celebration, an old European custom.' "[12]

Once Camp Crystal City was established, the government decided it had an obligation to educate the children. Four schools were built, and a Supervisor of Education was hired. A nursery and kindergarten were established as soon as the camp was open. The stated purpose of the government in establishing an education program and the schools was "to enable the children not to lose any time in schoolwork."

The government built a native language school for each ethnic group since many of the children would be returning to Germany and Japan with their families. Internees served as teachers, and educational procedures and class organization were left up to them, subject to the administration's approval and sanction of subject matter.

For the children whose parents contemplated remaining in the United States following their internment, the administration agreed to open an official school based on the Texas education system. This school was open to enrollment by any child, German or Japanese, who desired to continue or begin an American education.

The German school consisted of four rooms and an auditorium and was housed near the medical clinic in the community building. It had an opening enrollment of 250 students, and by the time the Germans were transferred to other camps, the school had a population of 420 students.

Due to the extreme shortage of teachers across the United States, and particularly in Texas, it was difficult to recruit qualified personnel for each of the schools. Some teachers were reluctant to accept a teaching position because they didn't know how long the job would last. Despite these obstacles, the superintendent was able to hire degreed teachers with previous experience in the public school system.

When the schools opened, the school administrator faced a problem that was unique to Crystal City. Every child was a transfer.

A few students had report cards and transcripts from the schools they'd previously attended, but the majority of them didn't. Students were placed in each grade according to what they told the school administrator.

Transcripts were requested from each student's school of record and less than one percent was demoted for misrepresentation. In many instances, transcripts were late in arriving. A senior high school girl from Hawaii didn't receive hers until one week before graduation.

During the first year of operation, school spirit was totally lacking and extra-curricular activities were hard to develop. The children resented having to attend classes, and there weren't any school traditions. The students were strangers to each other and to the faculty, and make-up work took too much time away from their families.

The Officer in Charge (OIC) saw that sporting events were the best way to develop school spirit. He came to this conclusion when he saw a football game between two groups of Japanese internees. The boys had a lot of energy, but no coaching and few football skills. The game ended without either side making a touchdown.

The OIC consulted with the Japanese and arranged for a game. Since most of the boys on one team attended the high school, the Supervisor of Education organized a high school team. The opposing team was made up of boys from the Japanese internee population. Staff members with previous experience agreed to coach the teams.

Edward Adams was the head coach for the Black team. He had coached high school and junior college teams in Kansas and played varsity football for the University of Illinois. Coach Adams said of his team: "I want my team to win of course, but regardless of the outcome, I hope that all players will let the spirit of good sportsmanship govern their actions throughout the contest."[13]

The head coach for the Orange team, R. C. Tate, had fifteen years' experience coaching high school teams at Devine, Uvalde, and Crystal City high schools. Coach Tate commented, "Regarding today's game, I am much more interested in how my boys play the game than in the final outcome of the game itself."[14]

No one would have believed they were in an internment camp for the big game. It was like a Friday night football game in any small town. A drum and bugle corps provided the music, and each team had its own pep squad to cheer them on. More than a thousand people came to watch. They sat in the stands and consumed hotdogs and drinks while cheering on their favorite team. At halftime, the drum and bugle corps came out on the field and performed to the cheers of the raucous crowd. Just like the first game, this one also ended in a tie.

The Germans preferred soccer to football and organized four teams that played against each other. The Japanese were never able to field a team to play against them until the Japanese internees from Peru arrived in camp. This team was young and very fast and they won more games than they lost.

With the passage of time, the high school sponsored picnics for the student body, the junior-senior prom, dances, and a school yearbook called *The Roundup*. The grammar school and the high school had commencement exercises with all of the usual programs. Each graduate was presented with a diploma. High school graduates wore caps and gowns.

The Texas State Board of Education inspected the schools and granted full accreditation for all courses taught. Some graduates eventually did go on to college. The valedictorian of the first graduating class was admitted to the College of Pharmacy at Texas University. Five more seniors enrolled at Texas University and a postgraduate student was accepted to Wayne University in Detroit, Michigan.

Music played a major role in the daily lives of the internees. The Germans and the Japanese each had their own musical groups. They played everything from the most popular songs of the day, to classical, to western, to their own ethnic music. The Germans thought some of the Japanese music was weird and the instruments they played were strange. The Japanese probably thought the same thing of the Germans. The Germans had a brass band and musicians and singers trained in classical music. The all-time favorite song of the internees was "Don't Fence Me In."

Medical care for the internees was a major concern for the administration. When the camp opened in 1942, the medical staff consisted of two nurses from the Public Health Service. To handle the needs of the first arrivals, a two-room clinic was set up in the only large building on the premises. The rooms were furnished with two small homemade tables, a wooden bookcase, and four folding chairs. Supplies were limited to a twenty-five-cent first aid kit, two pairs of scissors, and the personal property of the two nurses.

While waiting for a doctor and additional staff to take over operation of the clinic, the administration called on a physician and a dentist from Crystal City. By February 1943, cotton, gauze, adhesive, and a few drugs became available along with a few surgical instruments. The additional supplies and equipment made it possible for the staff to suture small wounds, open abscesses, and remove splinters. Later that same month, an internee physician, a number of voluntary internee workers, and six untrained female nurse's aides were added to the staff.

The first test of the clinic to handle a major epidemic came with the arrival of 112 Germans from Costa Rica. They entered the camp with forty cases of whooping cough and an epidemic of impetigo. Fortunately, the camp wasn't crowded yet. The medical staff was able to isolate the entire group and keep the epidemic from spreading to those already in camp.

To ensure they were ready for the next epidemic, the medical staff inaugurated classes for the nurse's aides. The nurses instructed the girls in clinical procedures and bedside nursing, but without the necessary equipment and charts to illustrate the lectures and techniques, it was an almost impossible task.

The staff encountered another problem once they received the supplies and equipment needed to keep the clinic in operation. Until construction on the new seventy-bed hospital was completed, supplies and equipment had to be stored wherever there was room. Staff and patients could hardly enter the clinic because of the large number of boxes stacked up on every inch of available floor space.

By May 1943 the staff was able to move into the completed part of the hospital. However, they exchanged one set of problems for another. The administration had situated the hospital in the middle of a field of cactus and mesquite. During the rainy season, the ground became a bog and the medical staff had to wade through knee-deep mud to get to the clinic. Extra shoes and stockings became standard issue. The situation was resolved with the construction of all-weather roads and sidewalks.

One day before the official opening of the hospital, a graduation ceremony was held for the first group of nurse's aides. Later that same month, additional nurses from the Public Health Service arrived, allowing the hospital to operate twenty-four hours a day. Once the hospital opened its doors, the staff consisted of five physicians, two dentists, one pharmacist, nurses, lab technicians, nurse's aides, orderlies, and janitors.

The administration was quick to acknowledge the cooperation and valuable service the internees rendered to the hospital. In the official record of Crystal City, the INS officer cited the example of the Japanese pharmacist who ran the hospital pharmacy.

> The Japanese pharmacist who dispenses drugs and medicines has an eye on the government pocketbook and a resultant economy that could not be excelled by an official employee. He frequently takes it upon himself to lessen the quantity prescribed by physicians, if he feels the patients might waste part of the medicine, telling them to bring back the bottle if a refill is needed. Another example is the tremendous quantity of lotion necessitated by excessive summer temperature here. This druggist has devoted hours to mixing the ingredients himself because the cost was considerably cheaper than if purchased in wholesale quantities. To date, some 30,000 prescriptions have been filled, which does not include medicines dispensed in the wards and in the clinic. Comparable work has been rendered by internee surgeons who have performed many major and minor operations.[15]

Before he was transferred to Ellis Island, Eberhard Fuhr traded his job on the ice truck for a job as an operating room orderly.

> I traded my job on the ice truck with the late Alfred Krakau for the job in the hospital as the Operating Room Orderly, but that was in 1946. The job entailed sterilizing all the instruments, gowns, gloves (were cleaned and reused) syringes, needles, sharpened too (no throwaways there), operating and OB packs and keeping the operating room ready for instant use in addition to the weekly OPERATING DAY schedule. The OB room was cleaned by someone else thank God, but the stuff used was done by me.

Dr. Martin of the U.S. Public Health Service was the Director. He was also the surgeon and on operating day he was really pumped, but always prepared with the specifics. He was short, in good condition, had I believe about five small children. He was probably about 35 years old. His staff was one German Doctor Kappus, two Japanese doctors (man and wife), a professional Nurse Corp from the USPH headed by his scrub nurse, Miss Clark, who really set the standards for sterile procedure matters for the OR and for the hospital. I believe there were about 5 other USPH nurses. These were augmented by nurses' aides of varying nationalities. There was also a USPH Dentist on staff.

All anesthesia was by spinal, except when time ran out when that was augmented by ether or chloroform drip on mask. There was a Cesarean while I was there and, since anesthesia was critical for mother and baby, Dr. Martin did the surgery.

Martin imported the Crystal City doctor along with a "gas anesthesia machine" to better control the levels involved. The Japanese doctors, may be named MORI would attend the baby when delivered. . . .

It was performed on a UK citizen married to a German from Honduras I believe, but memory can mislead. I remember Dr. Martin briefing each participant about the procedure . . .

The baby was delivered fine and the operation was fine, but we had difficulty in resolving recovery of all the sponges as the OR looked like a hurricane with all the discarded drapes, instruments, and whatever. The medical care was great in my opinion. The professionals never compromised and insisted on good practices.

In the winter of '46–47, about 100 Indonesian sailors who had mutinied in Los Angeles were brought to Crystal City. They were segregated and fenced off from the rest of the camp. Miss Clark advised me that I had to prepare a syringe tray for 60 sailors with syphilis. They would be injected twice weekly for six weeks with a sulfa drug. She advised me about being safe and protect myself, because the needles were reused after sterilization and sharpening. They too left CVC before I did.[16]

In July 1944, the camp was exposed to a second epidemic. A large group of internees from South America was infected with measles. Isolation was necessary, but the medical facilities were inadequate to handle the influx of infected prisoners. The medical staff quarantined them to victory huts, and for the entire time, outside temperatures averaged 112 degrees. Only one death resulted from this epidemic. None of the internees already in camp were infected with the disease.[17]

The medical staff did an excellent job of meeting the internees' health needs. There were the usual epidemics of influenza, strep throat, diarrhea, and other minor ailments. Stillbirths were numerous, and 255 babies were born to internees. The first birth was a Cesarean section performed in the downtown hospital. The first birth in camp occurred at home in the internee quarters, because the camp hospital hadn't been built yet. Due to the fact that records are unavailable, it isn't known how many deaths occurred while the camp was in operation.

NOTES

1. Representative Ciro D. Rodriguez, Tribute to Crystal City in Zavala County, Texas, Texas Congressional Record, December 19, 2007.
2. Joseph L. O'Rourke, Establishment and Construction of the Camp Historical Narrative, RG 85, Immigration and Naturalization Service, Crystal City Internment Camp, File 217/021, September 19, 1945.
3. Ibid.
4. Ibid.
5. Eberhard Fuhr, email to author, March 1, 2009.
6. John Schmitz, email to author, February 28, 2009.
7. Gunther Graber, email to author, March 2, 2009.
8. Eberhard Fuhr, email to author, March 4, 2009.
9. Arthur Jacobs, *The Prison called Hohenasperg*, Universal Publishers, 1999.
10. John Schmitz, email to author, March 13, 2009.
11. Eberhard Fuhr, email to author, March 4, 2009.
12. Arthur Jacobs, *The Prison called Hohenasperg*, Universal Publishers, 1999.
13. Edward Adams, head coach, Black Team, Crystal City Football Program, November 23, 1943.
14. R. C. Tate, head coach, Orange Team, Crystal City Football Program, November 23, 1943.

15. Eberhard Fuhr, email to author, March 9, 2009.
16. Eberhard Fuhr, email to author, March 14, 2009.
17. Louis Frist, "Medical Care for Interned Enemy Aliens, a Role for the Public Health Service in World War II," *American Journal of Public Health*, October 2003.

ELEVEN

MY INTERNMENT BY THE U.S. GOVERNMENT

Eberhard E. Fuhr

My parents, Carl and Anna, brought me to the U.S. in 1928 at the age of three. When I turned fifteen in 1940, I was required to register, along with all aliens over fourteen—male and female—complete with photo ID and fingerprints. In August 1942, the U.S. government interned both of my parents as German resident aliens. My twelve-year-old brother was interned with them even though he was an American citizen, having been born in Cincinnati. Had he not joined them, he would have been sent to an orphanage, a fate shared by other internee children.

Because my older brother was eighteen and I was seventeen, we were allowed to stay home and free, but had to fend for ourselves. My brother soon left for an Ohio college where he had an athletic scholarship. I lived alone. I went back to Woodward High in Cincinnati for my senior year. I continued to be active in student life, lettered again in football, participated in student clubs, and was even on the civil defense Bomb Squad.

I earned enough from my early morning newspaper route to survive. Periodically, an FBI agent would call to question me. Once they picked me up at 8:00 p.m., brought me to their offices, and questioned me for two hours under bright lights while toying with their guns. The questions concerned family friends, attitudes about relatives in Germany, and my parents' internment, what some neighbors (unnamed of course) were saying about me, and the like. I was being watched.

In January 1943, my brother dropped out of college and went to work in a Cincinnati brewery. On March 23, 1943, two FBI agents arrested me in class at Woodward High School. I was seventeen years old. When passing through school doorways, one preceded me with a drawn gun while the other held my arm. Outside the building, I was handcuffed. I never returned to school and did not graduate with my class just two months later. In fact, my picture was expunged from the yearbook except in team photos. I lost not only the belongings in my school locker, but also my dignity.

The FBI took me to my brother's place of employment, where he was arrested as well. We were then taken to the city police station, booked "on suspicion," fingerprinted, and transferred to the Hamilton County Workhouse. This was built in the mid-1800s and had a medieval look of turrets and very high walls. A five-tiered cellblock dominated the interior. Each cell was five feet by ten inches, with walls about one foot thick. Two chains held a metal bed from the wall, and a bucket served as a toilet. We were issued prison clothes without belts, and shoes without laces, and then locked in separate cells some distance apart.

Soon after the barred doors clanged ominously shut, prisoners began yelling vicious threats of what would happen to Nazis, Krauts, Huns, and other choice terms when the cells were opened in the morning. Fortunately, their bark did not equal their bite. In handcuffs, we were brought to the Federal Building for our hearings. Neither one of us was permitted witnesses or counsel. While my brother was in his hearing, I was graciously provided with coffee, an edible doughnut, and a copy of the *Cincinnati Enquirer*, which I should have been delivering. In shock I read, "Two Brothers Arrested. They will have a hearing and will be interned." Thus, prior to our hearings, the newspaper had been advised that we would be interned.

Following my brother's hearing, I had mine before the Civilian Alien Hearing Board and faced the same people who had interned my parents seven months earlier. There were five or six people on the board. One question concerned a statement I supposedly made about Hitler when I was twelve years old. I was questioned about attending German American Day at Coney Island in 1939 and 1940. They had eight-by-ten-inch glossy pictures of attendees.

Then I was asked what I would do if my German cousin asked me for sanctuary after landing with a U-boat on the Ohio River. I said something to the effect that a submarine would draught more than the river's depth, which precipitated a lot of irritation by the board. They went into raw data, which is really what anonymous informants call in as "evidence." It is impossible to refute because their anonymity is guaranteed, and I soon realized that anything I said would not be acceptable. I knew that we were to be sent to Chicago for internment. I had read it in the paper.

After the hearings, my brother and I were taken home on our way back to prison. We were advised to bring only enough clothes for about two days and to check that the doors and windows were locked. This was the last time we ever saw the house. The contents were later looted—pictures, stamp collection, violin, piano, furniture, keepsakes, and irreplaceable family memorabilia treasured by my mother—all gone and lost forever. The house was in foreclosure, as my parents couldn't keep up the payments without an income in internment.

We were returned to prison, reissued prison garb, and again locked into our separate cells. Early the next morning, we got our clothes back and assembled for the federal marshals to transport us by auto to Chicago. This time each of us was handcuffed to a ring on a belt buckled in the back. Additionally, we were then handcuffed together. During "rest stops," one of the marshals cuffed himself to one of us, forming a threesome that proved quite intimate while doing the necessary offices. Embarrassing is hardly the word.

We arrived late at night at 4800 South Ellis Avenue in Chicago. As we had eaten only one hotdog en route, one of the inmates gave us a sandwich from his personal stash, while the other inmates provided a warm welcome. We were there about three months. The population varied from about twenty up to thirty since some departed to internment in North Dakota or Texas and others arrived. The detention station itself was a turreted old mansion with a carriage house, surrounded by a cast iron fence. Two guardhouses had been added to the exterior. Because of the crowding in a building meant for a single family, the beds were metal army cots, and the only recreation was double pinochle. We were required to assemble twice a day for a physical count.

Ten days after my arrival, my eighteenth birthday required that I register for the draft. When I requested to be taken for that, the Detention Station Director advised me that I didn't need to register since I was now interned. I told him that the law applied to all who turned eighteen. After a ruling from his superiors, I was taken to the Cook County Jail Draft Board, which subsequently became my draft board for World War II.

In July 1943, we were taken to Crystal City, Texas, near Mexico, on a heavily guarded train with another thousand internees. The good news was that we were being reunited with our interned parents and younger brother. The bad news was that the fences were twelve feet high with guard towers every fifty yards in an area that was considered a harsh desert and home of scorpions, insects, lizards, snakes, and oppressive heat. Both incoming and outgoing mail was censored and limited.

In Crystal City, I met Japanese people for the first time. The internee population was split almost equally between Japanese and German, with one Italian. We shared the same facilities such as the hospital, school, and playing fields where we competed in basketball, fast pitch softball, and soccer. The only Japanese soccer team was composed of internees brought from Peru. Cultural events, though not restricted, were generally separate. They had their own music, and we had ours. They had sporting events peculiar to them and vice versa. We built a pool together that also served as an irrigation source for the region's farmers as well as the prison's farm. Diversity came along with Germans from Latin America. Many were married to wives indigenous to places like Panama, Costa Rica, Peru, Honduras, etc. Spanish, Japanese, and German languages could be heard throughout the internment camp in addition to English.

After VE Day, we thought we would soon be released, and after VJ Day, we were certain it would happen. However, it was not to be, because, apparently, President Truman wanted us all deported. Everybody except the Germans was released from Crystal City in 1946. In 1947, I was transported to Ellis Island for deportation to Germany, which I had left as a three-year-old.

Legal actions stopped that plan, proving that the system does indeed work. Following a hearing chaired by a Senate Judiciary

Subcommittee, I was released in September 1947, two and a half years after the cessation of hostilities in Europe. My family and I had to begin anew, but burdened with the stigma of internment. On the positive side, I met my wife in Crystal City and married her a year after release. We have three children and seven grandchildren. I graduated with honors from Ohio University and earned an MBA from the University of Wisconsin.

I was interned when I was seventeen and released when I was twenty-two. I did four and a half years' time for being German. Internment demonstrated to me the terror of governmental coercive power and the despair of hopelessness and interminable time. There was no end date. In addition to the stigmatization and humiliation, one wonders which "friend" gave damning "evidence" of what was said at the age of twelve.

Many bore the psychological scars throughout their lives. Many did not address their own families about internment, including my older brother, who only told his children just before he died. Like the Japanese, we need to tell our story, because we were not criminals but were caught in the same wartime hysteria that incarcerated the Japanese and Italians. We eleven thousand formerly interned Germans need to speak out so that this will not happen to anyone else.

While a sovereign nation has a right and a duty to protect itself, civil liberties should not be cast aside so freely, even in time of war. As a result of rumor and innuendo, families were torn apart and homes lost. No internee was ever convicted of a crime. Spies and saboteurs were not interned. They were, nevertheless, executed after receiving due process, which was not accorded to legal immigrants who were interned.

The Japanese story is well known due to the great work done by them. Are German Americans less deserving of recognition of the wrongs done them because of ethnicity? Are we not all equal under the law? Were the Germans, Japanese, and Italians not in the same internment camps together? It is time to acknowledge that Germans, German Americans, and other Europeans were indeed interned with the Japanese and Italians.

---- TWELVE ----

HAWAII

The arrest and detention of enemy aliens in Hawaii was in some respects much different from what the internees on the mainland experienced. A few hours after the attack on Pearl Harbor, Governor Joseph Poindexter issued a proclamation invoking the powers conferred on him by the legislature under the Hawaii Defense Act. The act gave him unlimited authority over inhabitants and their property along with the power to meet an emergency, limited only by minimum safeguards to the rights of the individual.

Later that same day Poindexter issued a proclamation placing the territory under martial law and suspended the writ of habeas corpus pursuant to Section 67 of the Hawaiian Organic Act that states:

> The governor shall be responsible for the faithful execution of the laws of the United States and the Territory of Hawaii . . . and he may, in case of rebellion or invasion, or imminent danger thereof, when the public safety requires it, suspend the privilege of the habeas corpus, or place the Territory, or any part thereof, under martial law until communication can be had with the president and his decision thereon made known.[1]

Governor Poindexter not only declared martial law and suspended the writ of habeas corpus, but he also exceeded his powers under Section 67 when he proclaimed,

> I do hereby authorize and request the Commanding General,

115

Hawaiian Department during the present emergency and until the danger of invasion is removed, to exercise all the powers normally exercised by me as Governor; and I do further authorize and request the said Commanding General during the present emergency and until the danger of invasion is removed, to exercise the powers normally exercised by judicial officers and employees of this territory.[2]

Concurrent with the issuance of the governor's proclamation, Lieutenant General Walter C. Short issued his own proclamation.

I announce to the People of Hawaii, that in compliance with the request of the Governor of Hawaii, I have this day assumed the position of military governor of Hawaii, and have taken charge of the government of this territory. I shall therefore shortly publish ordinances governing the conduct of the people of the Territory with respect to the showing of lights, circulation, meetings, censorship, possession of arms, ammunition, and explosives and the sale of intoxicating liquor and other subjects. In order to assist in repelling the threatened invasion of our island home, good citizens will cheerfully obey the proclamation and the ordinances to be published: others will be required to do so. Offenders will be severely punished by military tribunals or will be held in custody until such time as the civil courts are able to function.[3]

Governor Poindexter then informed the president that he had suspended the writ of habeas corpus, placed the islands under martial law, and turned all of the duties of his office over to General Short. Even though he had failed to consult with FDR and the Congress, the president approved his actions on December 9.

Over the next four weeks, the army issued 181 general orders. They covered everything from trials for felonies and misdemeanors to garbage collection, numbering of houses, food prices, rent, and even how much a prostitute could charge her clients. The orders forbade hiring, firing, quitting a job, or transferring to a new one without the express permission of General Short. Orders were issued without regard to territorial or federal laws and often ignored the precepts of the U.S. Constitution.

On December 8, an order was broadcast over the radio requiring all aliens to turn in guns, fireworks, cameras, short-wave receiving sets, and anything else that might be considered useful to the enemy to the nearest police station by 5:00 p.m. that afternoon. Anyone failing to meet the deadline was subject to "severe punishment." Some aliens dumped their valuables at the doors of the stations and hurried away without waiting for a receipt. Those aliens who turned their articles in after the deadline often refused to give their names.

An Alien Property Custodian took possession of the confiscated items and stored them in warehouses in various locations across the islands. Some of the articles deteriorated due to improper storage and handling, and those items that had souvenir value simply disappeared. Radios, binoculars, and telescopes were turned over to the Navy, and fireworks were used at jungle training centers to simulate battle conditions.

With the actions of Governor Poindexter and General Short, the door was open for the FBI to implement the detailed plans regarding the arrest and detention of Japanese, German, and Italian aliens, many of whom were American citizens. In a letter to the Director of the FBI, Special Agent in Charge, R. L. Shivers wrote:

> As soon as martial law was declared in Honolulu on December 7, 1941, by the Honorable Joseph Poindexter, Governor of the Territory of Hawaii, Lieutenant General Walter C. Short, Commander of the Hawaiian Department, through the Military Governor, Lieutenant Colonel Green, who had been appointed and designated as Military Governor by General Short, directed through the Military Governor and personally that all enemy alien Japanese and citizens of that ancestry be apprehended and interned on whom the Federal Bureau of Investigation had submitted custodial detention letters.[4]

As soon as the military governor issued the order for the arrest of enemy aliens, thirteen squads consisting of three FBI agents each, plus military personnel and local police officers, fanned out across the islands. Six squads operated outside of Honolulu, while the remaining seven operated within the city limits. The provost marshal was unable to provide the promised transportation for the raids, so the agents were forced to use their own personal vehicles. Agent Shivers also requested additional vehicles and manpower from the Honolulu police chief.

In Honolulu, the plan called for each squad to proceed to the meeting place in two cars equipped with two-way radios. Military police (MP) guards and a large army truck were to meet them there. Shivers stressed that the truck would not go to the scene of the arrest, but the prisoners were to be brought to the truck. Once a prisoner was loaded into the truck, the agent in charge received a signed receipt from the MP in charge. The truck proceeded to the Immigration Station in Honolulu to deliver the prisoners to the military police for internment.

In his report to J. Edgar Hoover, Agent Shivers described his actions in the raid on the aliens:

> The apprehension of these aliens went off much more smoothly with the use of personal automobiles than it would have if we had depended on the Army to furnish transportation as provided for in our plan. Three by five cards had been prepared previously on every custodial detention subject who was to be picked up, showing his name, address and citizenship status. It was therefore only necessary to give to each squad the cards on the subjects to be picked up in the districts to which they were assigned. These cards have been stamped on the back with the statement, "Received custody of the person named on the reverse side." I personally assigned squads to each precinct and beat and personally gave them the cards on the individuals to be apprehended, and personally gave them instructions regarding the apprehension of these individuals and their delivery to the immigration station so that the program could be expeditiously executed. As the individuals were picked up by the various guards, they were taken to the Immigration Station where they were receipted for on the reverse side of the card by the Military Police. The cards were then returned to this office.[5]

Under the supervision of the FBI, the Military Intelligence department and local police conducted the arrests of the aliens on the island of Hawaii. The prisoners were held at the Kilauea Military Camp at Kilauea, Hawaii. There were no agents on the islands of Maui, Molokai, and Lanai, and no way to get them there, so Army Intelligence was left to handle those arrests themselves. Fifty-one people were arrested on Maui, four on Molokai, and two on Lanai.

With the exception of Otto Kuehn, there is no record of any of the detainees committing espionage or sabotage in Hawaii. Kuehn was a German national who established residence in Hawaii several years before the war. His house was located across an alley from the home of the Japanese Consul General. This made it easy for him to transmit information to the Japanese.

Kuehn developed an elaborate system of signals to communicate information on ship movements in Pearl Harbor. This included lights from a beach house and a sheet on a clothesline at Lanikai; lights from a dormer window at nearby Kalama; markings on a sailboat in Lankai Bay; coded broadcasts over the KGMB radio station daily "want ads" program; and a bonfire on the slopes of Haleakala on Maui.

At his trial, Kuehn stated that he never intended to use the signals. He told the court that he drew up the plans for his signaling system in gratitude to the Japanese consulate for sending money to his stepson in Germany. Army intelligence reported there was no evidence the signals had ever been put into operation.

A military commission sentenced Kuehn to be hanged, but the Attorney General of the United States commuted his sentence to fifty years in prison, the maximum penalty for peacetime espionage. He was later released from prison and repatriated to Germany. On December 8, Kuehn's wife and daughter were working as volunteers at a first-aid station when they were arrested. They were interned for the duration, and at the end of the war, they, too, were repatriated to Germany.

After arrest, the next step was internment. The hearing board consisted of army personnel and civilian representatives. Regardless of the findings, the board could not intern or release prisoners without the approval of General Short or Colonel Green. As one member of the board stated:

> If the board orders the release of the subject, he cannot be released without the approval of the Military Governor or the Commanding General. If the Military Governor and the Commanding General decline to order his release, the subject must then remain in custody pending an appeal to the Secretary of War. The Commanding General and the Military Governor have

stated, "they will not release anyone, even though the board has ordered them released, unless approved by me."[6]

Family members left behind after the roundup had no idea where their loved ones were or whether they were alive or dead. The FBI refused to give out any information and would not allow the prisoners to communicate with anyone. Detainees were taken to FBI headquarters to be fingerprinted and photographed with an identification number as enemy aliens. During intense interrogations, the agents hurled outrageous accusations at the prisoners with no explanation of the charges against them. It didn't matter that some of the detainees insisted they were American citizens. As far as the FBI was concerned, they were enemy agents or worse.

After an initial interview, the prisoners were taken to Fort Armstrong Immigration Station. At the entrance to the station, they were dragged out of the cars and herded into the building by soldiers holding rifles with fixed bayonets. Husbands and wives were separated from each other and taken to separate holding areas. Each room was a large cell with iron bars that held forty to fifty people of all races and from all walks of life.

No one was charged with anything or given a reason for detainment. The arrests happened so quickly that the prisoners weren't able to bring anything except the clothes on their backs. They slept in army cots that were one foot apart from each other and there was only one sink and an exposed toilet. Detainees were kept incommunicado from the outside world. No telephone calls or any other types of communication were allowed.

Armed soldiers kept a nervous eye on their charges. With the way the soldiers handled their rifles, prisoners were afraid to ask too many questions for fear the guns might go off accidentally. It made no difference whether a prisoner was an American citizen or an alien. They were all treated the same—cursed and yelled at and condemned as Nazis, aliens, and spies.

A tribunal consisting of army personnel and local citizens heard each detainee's case. The board was anonymous, and the hearings were held in secret. Husbands and wives were questioned separately and not allowed to see each other. The prisoners did not have an attorney present as the board asked outlandish questions. They were not permitted to know the names of their accusers or where the accusations originated. The faceless accusers were never present, and the prisoners were denied the right to confront them.

By the middle of December, hearing boards consisting mostly of civilians were convened on each island. The boards were permitted considerable latitude in conducting the hearings. The Assistant Provost Marshal's Office provided a suggested board procedure, which said in part:

> It is desired that the hearing be confined to the pertinent issues involved in the internment, and cover the three subjects contained in the War Department directive, i.e., CITIZENSHIP, LOYALTY, and the INTERNEE'S ACTIVITIES . . . Character witnesses are of no value in a hearing of this type . . . The question of the internee's character is not particularly pertinent to these hearings . . .
>
> Keep in mind that these hearings are informal: that the internee is not heard as a matter of his rights and that it is desired that these records be expedited . . .
>
> Advise defendants that they may testify in their own behalf and that they may have counsel and that they may call witnesses, all at their own expense . . .
>
> Advise attorneys if they start an argument, it will not be allowed before the board.[7]

The hearings did not in any way resemble hearings in the judicial sense. They consisted mostly of reports of investigations and cross-examinations and lasted five or ten minutes. Doris Nye was a teenager when her parents were detained at Fort Armstrong.

> After his hearing, my Dad was told to sign the "findings" also he was a German Alien. He refused! The army officer put a revolver on the table. Dad laughed and said go ahead and shoot me. I will not sign and confess to lies. I am a U.S. citizen! (He was so proud to be an American!) Then the officer pointed the gun at his head. Dad continued to laugh and said go ahead and shoot me I refuse to sign that I am a German Alien." The officer replied, "Yes, but your wife and daughter are here also, first you, and then they." My dad signed.

My Mom was presented with her "findings" documents for signature from the "hearing board" including the fact that she too was branded as an alien. She refused adamantly stating that she was an American citizen. A gun was pointed at her head also. She finally signed, suspecting that if she did not, she would be shot. If the persons in charge, the FBI or military, had ripped her away from her home and children, incarcerating her in a cell, they would be capable of killing her. She would merely "vanish" without anyone knowing what happened to her. Finally, she signed.[8]

After two months of living hell at Fort Armstrong, the women were moved under heavy guard to Sand Island. They were confined to army barracks in one of three compounds built to house the prisoners. Each compound was surrounded by ten-foot-high barbed wire fences and patrolled by armed guards twenty-four hours a day. The first compound was for Japanese men, the second for German and Italian men and those of other races, and the third for women internees. There were two latrines, one at each end of the camp. Meals were eaten in a large communal mess hall. The men had been transferred to Sand Island weeks earlier and were already in their fenced areas. While the women lived in the barracks, the men lived in tents.

In February 1942, the men were taken from the camp and loaded into the hold of the U.S. Army transport *Grant* to Fort McCoy in Sparta, Wisconsin, via San Francisco. They were still wearing the same summer clothes they had on when they were arrested. The further east the prisoners traveled, the colder the weather. They stuffed newspapers in their shoes and shirts to keep warm. In the snow and freezing temperatures, they tramped through the gates of Fort McCoy.

The commander did his best to make the internees as comfortable as circumstances permitted. The army gave them warm clothes, blankets, heavy boots, and overcoats. On Saturday nights, the prisoners enjoyed a few beers while listening to music played by an internee band. On Sundays, an internee Lutheran minister conducted services for the men at a small chapel in the compound.

The internees from Hawaii might have remained at Fort McCoy indefinitely, but certain events transpired that forced the army to return them to Hawaii. The writ of habeas corpus hadn't been suspended in Wisconsin, and much to the army's discomfort, the internees took advantage of it. They wrote letters to anyone who might be able to help them.

As a result of their letter-writing campaign, the internees were able to contact a few lawyers who agreed to work pro bono to file writs on their behalf. One internee convinced a reporter for a local newspaper to write an article on the situation and how they were being held illegally. Before the article was published and the writs served, the army herded the internees onto trains and shipped them back to Angel Island. From there, they were loaded into the hold of a ship to Honolulu and reinternment at Sand Island.

Of all the internment facilities operated by the INS and the U.S. Army, the least-known camps were established in Hawaii. By war's end, an estimated 1,440 Japanese, Germans, and Italians had been interned on Oahu, Kauai, Maui, and the Big Island. Unlike the flat, sprawling compounds on the mainland, these camps were restricted to desolate, isolated areas or overgrown canyons far from the prying eyes of the island population.

Located on a five-acre island in Honolulu Harbor, Sand Island Detention Center was the first camp that all internees passed through. Originally constructed as an INS quarantine station, Sand Island was created from coral sand dredged up from the bottom of the harbor. It was a white gravelly material that packed easily and provided a shallow barrier to keep water from seeping through. During the rainy season, the soil had a tendency to puddle up on the surface, making the mud slushy from the coral dust.

Internees dug shallow ditches around the tents to drain off the water and planted beach grasses to reduce the heat from the sun. Pencils and paper weren't allowed, so they were unable to keep in touch with family members. Anyone caught attempting to smuggle messages out of camp was severely punished.

The camp was divided into two sections, one for the Japanese and one for the Germans. A ten-foot-high barbed wire fence, interspersed with guard towers and searchlights, separated the two camps. An aisle that ran between them made it easier to patrol. In addition to the other internees, a Japanese sailor who was captured when his mini-sub ran aground was held on that side of the camp.

For the first six months of confinement, internees were forced to live in tents until a limited number of barracks could be built. Depending on their circumstances, many of the internees lived in the tents until the camp was closed in 1943. According to all accounts, the tents were quite large but stood on bare ground, which created problems for the inhabitants. When it rained, mud was everywhere. The water puddled on the coral and ran sideways into the tents. The internees slept on army cots without mattresses and soon found their beds mired in the top layer of muck. When the sun emerged from behind the clouds, the mud dried and cracked. When the wind blew across the camp, everything was coated with fine particles of coral dust.

Every aspect of the internees' lives was controlled by the military. Eating, sleeping, mail call, and so forth were regulated by bugles just as in the army. There was the complete blackout for those living in tents. Go to sleep at twilight and wake up early at dawn to the harsh notes of a bugle. In the evenings, taps call was not sounded till later on, eight or nine o'clock. The barracks had blackout precautions so they could use their lights. Blackout windows were created by either painting all the windows black or by papering them with black tarpaper.

Detainees found different ways to keep busy. In addition to the daily physical exercises they were forced to engage in, they attended university sessions conducted by internees with expertise in specialized fields. A surveyor who knew a great deal about the stars lectured on astronomy. This was especially difficult because the internees couldn't leave their tents at night. Detainees lectured on such diverse subjects as the history of the Bible, Roman history, architecture, and shoe manufacturing. One musicologist taught classes on symphonies while another lectured on jazz. So many chefs from the finest hotels in Honolulu were picked up that food preparation became a major topic of study. The classes became known as the University of Sand Island or the College of Sand Island.

The guards for the mixed group compound (German, Austrian, Norwegian, Italian, and Swiss internees) were nothing more than young kids who had enlisted in the National Guard. Some of the guards were friendly, and since most of the Germans were American citizens who spoke excellent English, camaraderie developed between them. There were times when the guards were so exhausted they asked their charges if they could take a break and catch a nap in their tents. The Germans watched over them to make certain their superior officers didn't catch them sleeping on duty.

Even though the Germans were isolated from the outside world, the guards always gave them the latest war news. The Germans were extremely patriotic. They cheered when the Americans were victorious in battle and mourned when they lost. Even though their civil liberties had been denied, they were first, last, and always Americans.

Sand Island closed on March 1, 1943, and the internees were transferred either to camps on the mainland or to a new camp in Honoluilui Gulch in the Waianae Mountains. Built on 160 acres that overlooked Pearl Harbor, the camp was wedged between the Oahu Sugar Company fields and concealed in a wide gulch. Originally constructed to hold 3,000 prisoners, it never held more than 320 internees and some Japanese POWs.

Doris Nye was eleven years old when the Japanese attacked Pearl Harbor, but she has vivid memories of Camp Honoluilui:

> Camp Honoluilui was very isolated in the Waianae Mountains. It was huge and extended for quite a distance up the wide gulch. It held hundreds of individuals. For concealment purposes, it could not be easily seen from afar for its location was well hidden below the general lay of the land. Since no breezes reached it, the camp was HOT. To get to the campsite, one would have had to bump along a few miles mountainward from the old Kamehameha Highway using army vehicles, jeeps and trucks, to travel the dusty or muddy (depending on the season) newly bulldozed road. Unlike the cleared campsite, the surrounding areas were overgrown with dense low brush, much lantana, castor bean bushes, interspersed with stands of Kiawe trees and tall grass. At dawn, one could hear the twittering chorus of millions of birds. Outstanding among them were the myriads of red-feathered "Cardinals." They would hop about the camp or sit on the barbed wire fences and whistle their songs. Today, every time I hear the song of a red cardinal, my thoughts are bittersweet and return to Honoluilui. For even though my parents were incarcerated, every second we spent with them on weekends was packed with love and quality time.[9]

The camp was ringed with double barbed wire and patrolled by armed soldiers. Like Sand Island, it was divided into three separate compounds, one for the Germans, one for the Japanese, and one for the POWs captured in the South Pacific. Depending on their situation, internees lived in wooden barracks or tents. Unlike Sand Island, the tents had wooden floors. Using their own money for supplies, the men built porches with canvas awnings. To supplement their diets, the internees planted vegetable gardens in front of the tents. Family members were allowed two visits with internees each month.

The heat at Honoluilui was almost unbearable. The sides of the tents could be rolled up to let in a breeze, but the blistering rays of a Hawaiian sun and the excessive humidity turned them into saunas. To find some relief from the heat, the men stripped to the waist. They earned ten cents an hour working around the camp, and in their free time carved bowls out of monkey pod wood. The women kept busy sewing dresses from material they purchased from the Post Exchange (PX) on the Japanese side of the camp.

Almost everything was on the Japanese side of the camp: the doctors, the dentists, the PX. Doris Nye described one of her visits there.

> Sometimes I would get a pass to go over to the Japanese side of the camp. Everyone was so nice and friendly there. I remember seeing a dentist office run by an American Japanese dentist. However, I liked the PX the best because it sold delicious goodies. I came away with a bunch of candy bars that I bought. I had to use script that the internment camp issued to the internees. When visiting the Japanese side of the camp, I needed to pass the barbed wire enclosure that contained the Japanese prisoners of war. They had short cut hair and wore loincloths and they had pup tents for shelter. They certainly did not look like the parents of my Japanese friends but looked foreign. As I passed their enclosure, they looked at me with fierce looks. I ran.[10]

Martial law ended on October 24, 1944, but for the internees, imprisonment lasted for several more months. Because there is so little information available, the truth about the arrest and detention of American citizens of German, Italian, and Japanese ethnicity in Hawaii may never be fully known.

NOTES

1. Enforcement of Law, Hawaiian Organic Act, April 30, 1900.
2. Governor Poindexter, Proclamation, December 7, 1941.
3. General Short, Proclamation, December 7, 1941.
4. Letter from Special Agent Shivers to J. Edgar Hoover, December 7, 1941.
5. Ibid.
6. Doris Berg Nye, *The War Years*, January 11, 2009.
7. Ibid.
8. Doris Berg Nye, *Internment of U.S. Citizens of German descent,* January 11, 2009.
9. Ibid.
10. Ibid.

THIRTEEN

INTERNMENT OF A GERMAN-AMERICAN FAMILY IN HAWAII

Doris Berg Nye

My parents and my older sister were interned in Honolulu. The FBI took my dad, Fred Berg, and my mom, Bertha Berg, away on December 8, 1942. My older sister, Eleanor, age nineteen, was taken seven days later. My younger sister, Anita, age nine, and I, Doris, age eleven, were left as abandoned children. All five of us were United States citizens of German ethnicity. The internment and all of its ramifications were not supposed to happen to us. After all, as U.S. citizens, the federal Constitution, its freedoms, civil liberties, and certain "inalienable rights" protected us. But that was not the case. On December 7, 1941, the Constitution went out the window. Our American citizenship and our Constitution did not protect us after the attack on Pearl Harbor.

For years, we could not talk of the internment. The pain was too great and the injustice was too horrible to contemplate. My sisters and I did not speak of our past experiences during the war. Neither did we speak about it to our mother, who would have become upset. All of our experiences from December 7, 1941, through August 1943 remained buried. It was a lot easier to pull the coverings over our festering emotional wounds and pretend that all was fine rather than risk opening a Pandora's box and expose the horrific, heart-rending pain associated with the events. So no one talked.

Dad was born in Cologne, Germany, in 1902, and graduated

from the University of Cologne with a diploma in Commercial Science and Economics. He did post-graduate studies at the Universities of Munich and Nuremberg. He became a U.S. citizen in Hawaii in 1940. My two sisters and I were born in Honolulu, Territory of Hawaii.

My mother's parents emigrated from Germany in 1881 and were among the first contingent of German workers for Lihue Sugar Plantation. The youngest of five surviving children, Bertha was born in 1897. In 1914, she was pushed into an arranged marriage in Lihue with a German Alien—a legal long-time resident of Kauai. As a result of the marriage, she lost her U.S. citizenship. My sister, Eleanor, was born eight years later.

My mother despised her husband. She divorced him in 1927 and sailed for Europe. On the transatlantic trip, she met my dad, Fred. He had been sent to the U.S. to observe the Ford Motor Company's new assembly line process for his father, who was a wealthy industrialist in Germany. Also, Fred had been a student at the Packard Automobile Company in Detroit. After a year's study and a sightseeing trip with two friends in an old Model A touring car to the coast of California and back, he was returning to Germany with the intention of opening a Packard agency in Germany.

Mom and Dad were married in Dusseldorf on December 15, 1928. My father was the oldest son and heir to my grandfather's industries. He denounced all of his privileges to follow the woman he loved. By mid-October of that year, Dad and Mom, who was seven months pregnant with me, left Germany. Mom wanted her child to be born in America. Against her doctor's orders, my parents sailed for the United States.

Their intention was to return to Hawaii and make it their permanent home. Mom entered the U.S. under the non-quota law and Dad on a one-year visitation visa. After six months in Hawaii, he was forced to return to Germany. He cut his ties with his family and reentered the U.S. as an immigrant.

I was born at home in Kaimuki, Honolulu, Hawaii, on January 6, 1930. My little sister, Anita, was born two and a half years later.

In 1930, Congress passed a new law stating that a woman did not automatically lose her U.S. citizenship when she married an alien. Mom applied immediately and in July 1930, her U.S. citizenship was restored. After a vigorous examination and legal mix-ups due to ignorance of the law, Dad received his citizenship in 1940.

In 1938, our grandparents in Germany asked my older sister, Eleanor, to visit them, which she did. With thousands of other refugees and her Jewish fiancée who was an American citizen and a journalist for a New York newspaper, she escaped from Nazi Germany in 1940. After a short stay in New York, Eleanor was back in Hawaii by 1941.

Starting with twenty patients, in 1935 my parents opened the first private nursing home in the Territory of Hawaii. Their place of business was a large three-story home that they leased. The rooms of the residents were on the first two floors, and we slept on the third floor. One day around November 1940, one of our residents approached Mom and said that "so and so," who had a bedroom on the second floor directly beneath my parents' bedroom on the third floor, was reporting information to the FBI. Mom laughed and said, "Don't worry. That is okay. We are American citizens."

Mom didn't give the conversation much thought. Also, that resident on the second floor who was supposedly reporting us often acted inappropriately. He was an alcoholic with apparent brain damage. Who could possibly believe his gross hallucinations? Mom wasn't concerned.

On Sunday, December 7, I was in my parents' bedroom on the third floor. My dad was reading the Sunday comics to me. Suddenly, there was a loud explosion that rocked our home on its foundation. I leaped up and peered out of a window. Pearl Harbor was partially hidden under a huge, ominously dense cloud of black smoke. Dad said that maybe one of the many oil storage tanks at Pearl Harbor had caught fire.

I dashed downstairs to where my Mom was fixing breakfast and turned on the radio. A harried announcer was declaring, "This is the real McCoy. Pack food and clothing. Be prepared to escape to the hills. I repeat, we are under attack by the Japs!"

In answer to my question, Mom replied, "Yes, start packing food and blankets." Oh boy, I thought, we'll be camping out! I hauled out two empty cardboard boxes and began to fill one with food and the other with warm blankets. As I was packing I heard the scream of airplanes. My little sister, Anita, and I ran outside. Right above us, there was a group of Japanese Zeros and two American planes in a dogfight. One Japanese plane was shot down. Anita and I jumped around shouting, "Hooray for our side." Mom yelled for us to get in the house.

Our home was located in upper Liliha in Nuuanu Valley, right under the flight path of the attacking Zeros. There were more explosions. Later we found out that the Japanese not only bombed Pearl Harbor, but also Honolulu. Anti-aircraft shells exploding on the ground caused other explosions.

We kept the radio turned on to one of Honolulu's two stations that remained in operation. The announcer read out civil defense orders between long silences. Both Mom and Dad dealt with the residents and their relatives. That evening, we observed all of the new orders: "Stay off the streets. Keep your lights out. There is a complete blackout for all of the Territory of Hawaii. Anyone not complying will be severely punished. Any lights showing will be shot out!"

We went to bed early. Honolulu was waiting for the second attack. As a child, I felt as a child. Mom and Dad were there. I felt safe. I had always been a very active tomboy. Secretly, I thought this was exciting. Perhaps we would camp out in the mountains. I had no clue as to the real horrors of combat. The next day, Monday, December 8, 1941, my innocent senses would be violently shocked and reshaped by the black reality of war.

On that day, Dad abided by the order for all personnel to report to work. Dad's second job was at Sears. He left as soon as he heard the announcement on the radio. Barricades at the storefront needed to be constructed.

That same morning, many of the families drove in to remove their relatives from our nursing home. I waited in the yard to intercept requests for my mom. In the early afternoon, a black car pulled up with two men in it. They looked like Elliot Ness types with hats and suits. I thought they were members of a resident's family. They asked to see my mom and I told them to wait while I got her.

I dashed up the back stairs to the kitchen and to my disbelief, the men raced right behind me. I found Mom. They started talking.

She asked if she could put on some lipstick. I was horrified when they followed her right into the bathroom. My eyes were as big as saucers. I could see that one had a revolver. When they emerged, she said to me, "Doris, these men want to ask me some questions. Take care of your sister and the patients and I will be right back."

The hours went by and she did not return. That night I waited out on the porch. I listened to the silent radio, spinning the dial, trying to find some information, bulletins, police conversation, anything. Dad hadn't returned either. I knew that something horrible had happened to them. An accident? I watched anxiously. Occasionally a car would creep slowly up the street in the dark. The hours went by and none of the cars stopped.

Later, I heard shouting and gunshots coming from the street. Someone had turned on a light. I thought it was one of the residents. Rushing into the kitchen, I saw that it came from the third floor. Up the stairs I ran, screaming, "Turn off the light!" I heard more gunshots. I lunged for my little sister and the light switch in one swift motion. Anita forgot it was a blackout. I was terrified, apprehensive, and sick with worry. I was not gentle. How could I be?

Then I dashed back down the stairs and onto the porch. Around eleven o'clock that night, knowing that Mom and Dad would never willingly leave me in charge of the patients, my fears began to crystallize and a ghastly sense of realization, shock, and resignation invaded my thoughts. They were never coming home. How could they? The two men must have killed them. Both Mom and Dad were dead.

By the next afternoon, our help had left. Anita and I were alone except for some patients who had not gone yet. I was near shock, but I had to keep everything together and control my emotions. Mom relied on me. I have snatches of memory of making some pancakes for those who were hungry. That afternoon, there was a low-key party, as if a small group of people were toasting my parents' departure. I heard low whispering interspersed with soft laughter. It was so inappropriate at the time. They didn't know that Anita and I were sitting nearby on the inside stairs, concealed in the shadows.

After my parents were gone, all kinds of people walked into our home. Some came into the kitchen and took our food. I didn't know who they were. A few of the men may have been FBI agents looking for "secret spy evidence." I hadn't seen them before. I tried to help those who asked questions. Regarding my parents, I simply said, "They are not home now. They had to go to town." I tried to keep calm. That was the hardest part. I couldn't fall apart and appear like some sniveling child, which was exactly how I felt on the inside. Every raw emotion was screaming in terror! I held it in with an invisible black robe of calm and resignation.

Approximately one week later, my older sister, Eleanor was driven into the yard. She had been on Molokai visiting with my favorite aunt. Anita and I were elated to see her. We told her what had happened, that we thought Mom and Dad were dead because they had just vanished. I was so relieved to have Eleanor back. Now that sense of responsibility was off my shoulders. She would take care of everything. I didn't have to act like an adult. I could be a kid again. However, my sense of relief was soon shattered.

Our car was still in the garage. That same day Eleanor drove us down to Piggly Wiggly to buy some food. We found there wasn't much left to buy. On the Monday after the attack on Pearl Harbor, the military governor had shut down all the food stores for inventory. A few days after the attack, they were allowed to open again.

The next day, December 16, I was in the yard petting my precious best friend, my cat Kitty Poo, and feeling somewhat like a kid again when the same thing happened once more. Déjà vu! A black car drove into our yard with two men dressed like Elliot Ness. This time they asked for Eleanor. A bolt of shock slammed through me. "Not again!" I screamed. I lost it. Hysterically shrieking, "Nooooo! Nooooo!" I raced up the back stairs, up the next flight, and up to the third floor. Eleanor was in our bedroom on the third floor sorting clothes.

I shoved Eleanor into the attic to hide her—anything so those killers wouldn't get her—but they were right behind me. I screamed, "Elle, they're going to kill you, too." I beat the men with my fists as they pulled her away and took her down the stairs. All the while I screamed, "Don't take our sister! Don't kill her like you killed Mommy and Daddy! Take us and kill us, too! Don't leave us here!" I beat at them and scratched them and bit them ferociously as they led her across the lawn and into the car. They peeled my fingers off the car window and then slowly drove off.

My whole world collapsed. I threw myself on the ground, screaming and pulling the grass up in chunks. A *third* one would be murdered! After a while there were no more tears left. I pulled myself together. I had to think. I still had my little sister to take care of. I needed to keep her safe, but where could we go? Finally, I decided. My aunt—my mother's sister—on the Island of Molokai would take us. She was always very good and kind to me and I had always loved her.

A few hours later the telephone rang. I ran to grab it. It was my sister, Eleanor. I asked her, "Where are you?" She replied, "I can't say." I said, "Have you seen Mommy and Daddy?" She said no and then asked if we were okay. I said yes. I didn't know who might be listening. Then she asked, "Where will you go?" I told her that I would take Anita and go to Molokai. She then told me that she had to go and hung up.

Suddenly, I had hope. If Eleanor was still alive, then maybe, just maybe, Mom and Dad were alive too. I stopped to think. We couldn't go to Molokai. We needed to stay right there in case Mom and Dad did come home. They wouldn't find us if we were gone. Perhaps someone would still return home today. I began to hope again.

Meanwhile, unbeknownst to us, Mom and Dad were being held at Fort Armstrong Immigration Station. They were first taken to FBI headquarters to be fingerprinted and have "mug shots" taken as aliens. Although my parents kept insisting that they were American citizens, they weren't believed. Outrageous accusations were hurled at them. After the FBI finished with them, my parents were led at gunpoint into a car and driven to Fort Armstrong.

They were met by nervous young men there, holding loaded rifles tipped with bayonets, who herded them into separate large holding areas. Mom was taken to a room with thirty-five to forty other women of all races and walks of life. Dad was put in with the men, which included all of the Japanese men who had been arrested on December 7.

At first, the Japanese thought the Germans were spies put in with them to gather information. They soon realized that this was not the case. Mom kept asking why she was being treated like this.

Her guards shouted at her, "You are an alien Nazi." She didn't want to argue too much with them because the way they were handling their rifles. She was afraid that they might accidentally go off. It was an experience of bewilderment and horror. She was worried sick about her children and all of the residents of her nursing home. She could only resort to prayer. It was Monday, December 8, 1941.

One of the other women who had been picked up screamed all night. The FBI men told her to leave her baby and that she would be right back, but of course she wasn't. The next morning, a doctor was called in to treat her, and before long she disappeared. Mom didn't know whether she was released or not.

Eleanor told a more detailed account of how she was taken on December 15, 1941. Two FBI men, who showed her their identification and said that she should accompany them to their offices for questioning, confronted her. Eleanor could not forget her screaming and hysterical sisters. On arrival at the FBI headquarters, she was fingerprinted and photographed with an identification number as an enemy alien.

After several hours of a harassing "we don't believe you" style of questioning, Eleanor was ordered to get into a car and told, "You are a prisoner, an enemy alien, and will be detained." She knew she was a U.S. citizen, and no one told her what law she had broken or under what specific charge she was being detained. Eleanor was first allowed to make the telephone call to us. Two FBI agents then drove her to Fort Armstrong where she was turned over to a soldier. With the bayonet of his rifle pressed into her back, he marched Eleanor up a flight of stairs and turned her over to a matron. She was searched and locked in a large ward-type barred room with thirty-five or forty other women. It was in this ward that she was reunited with our mother.

No one knew why they were detained. No one had been officially charged with a crime, nor were they allowed to bring anything with them. No one had a change of clothing. Their army cots were one foot apart, and there was one exposed toilet and one sink. There was no privacy. They were not allowed contact with anyone on the outside. Eleanor learned that our dad and her birth father were being held in another ward with a large group of men of all racial backgrounds. At night, there were no lights except for the brief flare of matches from those who were lighting cigarettes.

On December 20, 1941, Mom had her hearing in front of a tribunal consisting of army personnel and some local citizens, all of whom remained anonymous. Everything was very secretive. Unlike the detainees on the mainland, they were not allowed to have a lawyer present. Dad and Eleanor had their hearings at around the same time. Each was interrogated separately and asked outrageous questions. They weren't permitted to see each other or to confront their accusers. The names of the accusers were withheld and they were not present in the hearing room. It wasn't until years later that we learned the identities of the informants who had accused Mom and Dad.

Mom was kind and loved by everyone except three persons with an ax to grind. Two of the informers were residents of our nursing home, and the third was a former employee. The first one was a renowned troublemaker. Because it was in his hospital records, Mom knew that he had been expelled from many facilities, but she thought she could make a difference. The second one was an alcoholic. According to doctor's orders, he was not supposed to drink for fear of his liver rupturing. Mom enforced the orders and kept him from drinking. He was furious. The third one, an employee, was a woman who had acted inappropriately toward the residents and was fired.

Another accuser was a man who worked with my dad. This man was always spouting off about how great Hitler was. Dad hated Hitler and considered him a degenerative rabble-rouser. Also, some of Dad's coworkers were envious of him. Since he came from the German elite, Dad was a gentleman with impeccable manners and extremely friendly. The informer was jealous and took it upon himself to report Dad to the FBI.

Mom and Dad were cross-examined and accused of espionage and of conducting Nazi meetings in their bedroom. My father was asked repeatedly, "Why did you seek employment at the German Embassy? Did you work at Pearl Harbor to spy on the U.S. military?" Dad replied that these accusations were insane. My parents didn't know what they were guilty of—they were never charged with anything. Statements were read to them and questions asked, and that was that.

According to the transcript of my parents' case, the interviews lasted five to ten minutes. Mom seemed to be in a state of numbness because the questions asked of her had to be repeated over and over again. After his hearing, Dad was ordered to sign the findings of the board that he was a German alien. When he refused, an army officer placed a revolver on the table. Dad laughed and said, "Go ahead and shoot me. I will not sign and confess to lies. I am a U.S. citizen." He was so proud to be an American. The officer then pointed the gun at his head. Dad continued to laugh. "Go ahead and shoot me, but I refuse to sign that I am a German Alien." The officer replied, "Yes, but your wife and daughter are here also. First you, and then them." My Dad signed.

The hearing board presented Mom with her findings documents for signature. They branded her a German alien. She refused to sign, stating adamantly that she was an American citizen. A gun was also pointed at her head. She finally signed, suspecting that if she didn't, she would be shot. If the persons in charge, the FBI or military, had ripped her away from her home and children, incarcerating her in a cell, then they were capable of killing her. She would merely vanish without anyone knowing what happened to her. Finally, she signed.

Eleanor was not presented with a confession to sign at that time, but later, just before she was released in April 1942. She was handed several documents and told to sign them. Eleanor wanted to read the documents and was told not to. "If you want to go home," they said, "sign." She did. One document ordered her under pain of re-detainment never to say a thing about what had transpired. She was also told to report to an army parole officer once a month until the end of the war. Any violation of her parole would ensure an immediate return to the camp.

Not one of my family's so-called confessions was signed voluntarily. Yet those documents are still on their records in Washington, DC, today. Even though recently released documents show Mom, Dad, and Eleanor as U.S. citizens, they are still listed as aliens on the records. Notwithstanding they signed under coercion, these lies continue to be proclaimed as truths and given as reasons for their months in those "hell holes."

Around the time of the hearings, all of the women were moved from Fort Armstrong to Sand Island under heavy guard. There, three compounds had been set up, each surrounded by two high barbed-wire fences. The outer fence was interspersed with guard towers and spotlights. The men were already in the fenced areas. A few at a time had been removed from their side of the immigration station and disappeared. The remaining detainees didn't have a clue what had happened to them. Were they released? No, as tents became available, the remaining men were also transferred to Sand Island. There they were separated into two compounds, one for the Japanese and one named the "Miscellaneous" or "Mixed Group" compound for Germans, Italians, and men of other races. The third compound, a large barracks type of building, was for the women, including Mom and Eleanor.

A week after my parents were arrested, Mom was told that since she and Dad owned valuable property, she must sign a power of attorney over to a Mr. Reed, a casual acquaintance, or the government would confiscate it. What choice did she have? So she decided to allow the FBI to contact Mr. Reed, who was a used car salesman and sometime realtor. Unwillingly, she signed the document. In another part of the building, Dad signed too.

Around December 21, 1941, Anita and I went to live with our Aunt Anna. She wasn't too happy about it. We weren't allowed to say who we were or to speak to any of the neighbors. My aunt told everyone that we were war refugees. I couldn't blame her. As U.S. citizens of German descent, she and her family were possibly under surveillance and afraid for their own safety.

A few days before Christmas, Mr. Reed came by with a number of presents my parents had bought and hidden in the attic of our home. I saw a gift that for two years I had wished for—a jigsaw. I wasn't allowed to keep it. We were only allowed to keep two or three gifts (pajamas and panties), and all else was given to the Salvation Army.

Mr. Reed took us back to our three-story home to see if there were any clothes we could find. There was nothing. The house was trashed. Everything of value had been stolen. I saw my precious Kitty

Poo, my best friend. Happy to see me, she was purring around my ankles. I hugged her and held her close. Although I tearfully begged and begged, I wasn't allowed to take her with me. I had to put her down. No one would be there to feed her. I had to leave Kitty Poo to fend for herself.

I was overcome with grief. I sobbed and sobbed. It was as bad as leaving a loved family member forever, knowing that because you weren't there to provide food for them, they would starve and perish. Now a fourth loved one would die. The loss was devastating. That night I did something that I had never done before: I started to wet my bed.

One day in January, a woman came to Aunt Anna's house. The woman and my aunt were at the far end of the living room speaking in very low voices. After the woman left, my aunt gave me a letter. It was from Mom, written to me and Anita. I will never forget its smell of tobacco. The letter was written in pencil on the back of a laundry slip and appeared as if it had been folded very small and hidden in a pack of the woman's cigarettes in order to be snuck out. Apparently this was the second attempt to sneak out a message to us from Mom. Although she never talked about it, according to her released records, it was the first time she was caught and punished. I don't remember what was written in the letter, but it brought a sense of relief to know that she was all right.

Either from Aunt Anna or from the letter, we learned that Mom was being held at Fort Armstrong. I was always looking for hints as to where my parents might be and hoping they were alive. Now I had the name of a place. I tried everything to find a way to get down to the immigration station, but for their own security, no one wanted to take us. Finally, I threatened my oldest cousin that if he didn't take us, I would tell my aunt that he was secretly dating a Hawaiian woman, which was unacceptable by their family standards.

He gave in and drove us to the immigration station. We ran inside and I spoke to two women behind a desk next to a "No Trespassing" sign at the entrance to a long corridor. I explained that my mom and sister were possibly there and asked if we could visit them or if they could tell my mom we were there. They both professed ignorance. I found out later that Mom and Eleanor were a short distance down the hall. I was disappointed, but that didn't end my search.

On February 21, 1942, while we stayed with Aunt Anna, Mom and Eleanor were transferred to Sand Island. At the same time, along with a contingent of German and Japanese internees, Dad was loaded aboard the U.S. Army transport *Grant* and taken to San Francisco. The men disembarked and were shuttled under heavy guard to Angel Island, where they were held for a few days. They were then loaded onto trains, but no one knew where they were going. As the scenery became bleaker and the weather grew colder, the men stuffed newspapers into their shoes and shirts to keep warm. They were still wearing the same summer clothes they had on when they were arrested in December. The men arrived at freezing, snowbound Fort McCoy, Wisconsin in their thin, tropical Hawaiian clothes.

Dad said the military officials at Camp McCoy treated them very well. The internees were given warm clothes, blankets, heavy army boots, and coats for the cold. They attended chapel, and the Lutheran minister was one of the German internees from Wisconsin. The men were also given a few steins of beer on Saturday night while a band composed of members of the internees played. The commander was very helpful in making the U.S. citizens as comfortable as possible.

At Camp McCoy, Dad and others tried to convince the people in command that they were American citizens. At first, no one believed them. Dad complained of not having any money in his letters to Mom. He was envious of the mainland German aliens who received well-filled care packages from their relatives. He felt bad that he always had to borrow money to buy cigarettes, combs, razor blades, soap, and other necessities. Mr. Reed was supposed to send Dad money, but was pocketing it instead.

Now that Dad was out of the picture, Mr. Reed concentrated his efforts on trying to convince Mom to sell all of their property. In Dad's letters to Mom, he supported her efforts not to sell the property. Most of the relatives didn't know the men had been shipped out, but Mr. Reed was in touch with the FBI and knew where they were. Later, when the families found out where the men had been sent, they were able to send care packages and money. But for Dad, there was nothing. Mr. Reed did not tell us what happened to Dad, nor did anyone else.

Back at Sand Island, Mom heard that the men had been shipped out. She had no idea where Dad was until she received a letter from him in Wisconsin. She later learned that the wife of Dr. Zimmerman, an American citizen and internee from Hawaii who had been sent to Camp McCoy, had hired a lawyer. The lawyer was somehow able to secure a writ of habeas corpus through a Judge Metzger. In granting the writ, the judge had defied the army. When the writ was delivered to the Commander of Sand Island, General Emmons, he said, "I am sorry, but Zimmerman is not here."

According to Mr. Stephen Fox's book, *An American Gulag*, another attorney offered his services pro bono to the American citizens when they got to Wisconsin and was planning to file their writs of habeas corpus. Finally, one of the U.S. citizens at Camp McCoy was able to make contact with a lawyer friend in Wisconsin to file a writ of habeas corpus. Another internee got in touch with a newspaper reporter who was prepared to write an article on what was happening. Before the article was published and the writs served, the Hawaiian contingent was loaded on trains and sent back to Angel Island. From there, they were shipped back to Honolulu and internment at Sand Island.

After Eleanor's release and before my dad's return, Mom was found to have a large tumor. She was sent to St. Louis College in Honolulu for an operation. Anita and I caught a bus to go see her, but we weren't allowed inside. An army guard with a rifle stood in front of her room and stopped us. I tried to peek around him, but I couldn't see. The room was dark.

While at the hospital, Mom asked a Red Cross volunteer if she could have a piece of paper and a pencil to write to her children and let them know that she was okay. The woman replied that she did not give free items to Nazi spies and walked out of the room. However, a woman from the Salvation Army gave Mom a paper and pencil, and she did write the letter. We never received it. Because of the woman's kindness, Mom never forgot that organization.

When Mom was released from the hospital, she was supposed to take it easy. She had undergone quite extensive abdominal surgery.

The matron at Sand Island said that in no way would a Nazi get to take it easy. She made Mom mop floors and carry heavy buckets of water. Mom's unhealed stitches tore and she developed a hernia. She bound herself with a towel and safety pins, but did not dare tell anyone. She was afraid of what might be done to her next. Afterward, she wore a hernia belt until she was quite old.

Early in April 1942, my aunt had a heart attack. The same older cousin who had taken us down to the immigration station to see Mom threatened that we would be sent to an orphanage. He told me to run next door to get the doctor. I tried, but the doctor wasn't in—how was I supposed to know that the doctor was a dentist?

My cousin already despised my little sister and me, and now he was furious with us. He couldn't wait for us to leave and told Anita and me to pack for the orphanage, where we should have gone in the first place. The two of us stood in the kitchen with our arms around each other, crying. We were terrified of that orphanage. As Anita and I huddled there, I looked up. I couldn't believe my eyes. Like a guardian angel, there at the back door appeared our older sister, Eleanor. What a miracle. She had been released. We gathered our things and left. We three were on our own.

Because Eleanor was underage, she was not supposed to take Anita and me. It would have been a violation of Eleanor's parole if we were discovered. Petrified of being separated and sent to an orphanage, I hid our identity by lying. To lose my loved ones once more would have been devastating. After having been split up for months, I couldn't go through that again and was determined to keep us together through whatever scheme I could devise. I was growing up fast.

Four months after the attack on Pearl Harbor, Eleanor said we could visit our mom at Sand Island. It was a harrowing experience. A Navy launch waiting for passengers at dockside. On the launch, all of the visitors avoided looking at each other. Many looked down, including myself, perhaps from shame or fear. I didn't want anyone to know who I was.

We landed at the small wharf at Sand Island and had to walk over the white coral to the concentration camp, as we called it. As we got closer, I heard an unnervingly weird sound. It was the cries of the women in the camp. We could see them hanging onto the inside of the barbed-wire fence. The women had their arms outstretched to their loved ones whom they hadn't seen since the day they were interned.

What a joyful reunion. We walked through a baffled entry into a large mess hall barracks with darkened windows. We were allowed to sit with Mom on benches at the mess table. She introduced us to some of the other internees. The matron and the guards, who were located at each end of the dining room, watched us closely.

Our visit ended too soon. We had to walk back over the coral to the waiting launch. As the launch sailed away from the island, we waved and waved until we couldn't see our mother or the others anymore. Our Dad of course, wasn't there. Since February he had been at Camp McCoy in Wisconsin.

Around May 1942, the men returned from Camp McCoy and were reunited with their wives. The couples were moved to the women's side of the camp. They ate together in the baffled mess hall and slept in tents that were pegged down into the coral sand. Dad dug a trench around the perimeter to keep the rain from flooding their tent. For one year, the tent on the coral floor was their home.

Starting in June, Anita and I were able to visit our parents for a few weekends during our summer vacation. It was the first time we had seen our father since he was arrested on December 8. The days were quite hot, so Dad raised the flaps around the sides of the tent to let some fresh air in. One day a week, he had to make sure the ones on the windward side were lowered to keep the coral sand from blowing into the tent before the weekly inspection. The captain who ran the camp would walk through the tents with some other military men and conduct a "white glove inspection." I was told that when he walked through the tents and brushed the furniture or parts of the tents inside, the gloves needed to stay white, or the occupants would be punished.

All of the tents were meticulously kept—nothing like German "hausfraus" with their men to make sure everything was kept as neat as a pin. Even though they were unhappily incarcerated, they took personal pride in their fenced home, from the tents to the common areas, including the urinals.

Toward the end of 1942, my parents had a second hearing. This one lasted longer, and they were able to have an attorney present. He wasn't permitted to question the members of the tribunal or the accusing anonymous informers whose written charges were held by the tribunal. He could only question Mom, Dad, and Eleanor, who were requested to be present. Despite the fact that there were fifteen character witnesses including doctors, community leaders, and a judge attesting to my parents' loyalty as American citizens, the witnesses were not believed. The tribunal listened to all, but in the end based their entire judgment on the original wording "to be detained until the war is over," and the reports of the anonymous informers. Again, my parents were not allowed to face their accusers or to know who they were. My parents were American citizens with absolutely no rights.

By March 1, 1943, my parents were sent to Camp Honoluilui in the Waianae Mountains along with approximately thirty-five other Germans and one Italian. Camp Honoluilui also had three compounds, one for the Japanese, one for the Caucasians, and one for the Japanese POWs from the Pacific theater of war. By the end of March or the beginning of April 1943, we were able to visit Mom and Dad again on weekends.

Camp Honoluilui was very isolated in the Waianae Mountains. It was huge and extended for quite a distance up a wide gulch. The camp held hundreds of individuals. For concealment purposes, it could not be easily seen from afar, for its location was well hidden below the general lay of the land. Since no breezes reached it, the camp was hot. To get to the campsite, one would have had to bump along a few miles mountainward from the old Kamehameha Highway using army vehicles—jeeps and trucks—to travel dusty or muddy (depending on the season) newly bulldozed roads.

Unlike the cleared campsite, the surrounding area was overgrown with dense low brush interspersed with stands of kiawe trees and tall grass. Nearby, there were pineapple fields. At dawn, one could hear the twittering chorus of millions of birds. Outstanding among them were the myriad red-feathered cardinals. They would hop about the camp or sit on the barbed-wire fences and whistle their songs. Today, every time I hear the song of a red cardinal, my thoughts are bittersweet and return to Honoluilui. Even though my parents were incarcerated, every second we spent with them on the weekends was packed with love and quality time.

I noticed that the transfer to Honoluilui brought an upgrade to my parents' accommodations. This time their tent had a wooden floor. What a luxury! Again, Dad built a little porch with an awning for a roof. In front of the tent, he planted morning glories that he trained on strings. I planted a small vegetable garden that they tended. My parents lived there until their release: Mom in June 1943 and Dad in August 1943.

On our own, we girls had a difficult time. After leaving our Aunt Anna's home in 1942 with Eleanor, she was able to find a furnished two-bedroom house about a half-mile walk from school. Although she was working, it wasn't easy for Eleanor to pay rent and buy food, clothing, and all else out of her meager salary. In the summer of 1942, we moved to a small two-bedroom home in Waikiki. The rent was cheaper.

My clothes were becoming washed out and faded. There were many times when we were hungry. Fortunately for us, the home was convenient to the ocean. Also, there were three coconut trees in the front yard. Anita and I would go to the beach to hunt for edible seaweed to eat, or I would climb the coconut trees for the nuts.

Food was definitely an issue. Eleanor was able to find a job near the Army and Navy YMCA at an open-sided hamburger stand, "Swanky Frankie," perched on the busy corner of Hotel and Bishop Streets in Honolulu. Frequently, I would take the bus the short distance to where Eleanor worked. She would sneak me hamburgers for lunch and more for dinner. There were so many new songs that blared from the ever-running jukebox. I liked, "Oh, give me land, lots of land, under starry skies above. Don't fence me in." My thoughts were not of the Texas cattle, but the words were more appropriate for the internees behind their barbed-wire fences.

In the beginning of 1943, while we still lived in Waikiki, we became very short of money. To help pay the rent, Eleanor took in two women hula dancers with their four children. That made a combination of three adults and six children in a two-bedroom, one bath home. They rented Anita's and my room, and their children slept in the living room on a pair of comfortable twin couches under the windows.

Anita would take turns with the other children for a couch, but I, the oldest, slept on the living room floor. There was no carpeting. It was hard, and I learned quickly that sofa pillows did not stay put— they slipped all over the place during the night. I didn't complain.

Within a year, I was plunged from a happy, well-fed, normal, self-confident child in a hard-working, loving, and affectionate family to a traumatized, worldly grownup in a kid's body. I was all but a street urchin whose total being was thoroughly drenched with fear every waking minute—fear of discovery, detection, separation, and the orphanage. To heck with the luxury of one's own bed. I was living on survival instincts and skills. Having the three of us together under one roof was most important. If sleeping on the floor was what needed to be done, then it was acceptable.

By this time I had forsaken my long pigtails and let my hair hang freely. I had no bobby pins—an expense we couldn't afford. To hold my hair in place, I braided a coconut leaflet and wore it around my head like an Indian. Because it was Hawaii, I didn't need shoes or warm clothes. Actually, I looked like a street kid, and that was okay with me, as long as I blended in with the general population and wasn't singled out. At school, my friends were Japanese or local part-Hawaiian kids. With my dark eyes, tan skin, and long unbraided hair, I passed myself off as part Hawaiian also. Great! Anything to conceal my identity.

I had excellent kid communication skills—Pidgin English. I avoided anyone who asked questions, especially the mainland defense worker families of some of my acquaintances. A couple of moms didn't allow their children to play with me. Our home and its occupants were far from the conception of America's version of the perfect, apple pie family. When asked where my parents were, my standard answer was, "My dad is in the military and my mom followed him." I didn't say which side of the fence they were on.

Many times when I was in my chameleon role, I felt odd—fitting in, but not fitting in, especially when I remembered that I was German. I hated what the Germans were supposed to be. *My* family wasn't like that at all. We didn't belong to any German groups. We were baptized Lutherans but very spiritual without attending the German church. At night we said our prayers together. Aside from Mom's sisters, who spoke a variation of Hanover Platte Deutsch or Kauai German (as my Dad laughingly explained), there was no speaking German outside of the family. I was raised to be proud to be an American in a family that celebrated the Fourth of July by flying the American flag, watching fireworks, and attending military parades. I was torn, and I learned not only to hide my identity, but also my feelings behind a mask of cool calm.

In December 1942, our second Christmas without our parents was slowly approaching. For me it was a time of sadness. I didn't realize it, but I had slumped into depression. I hadn't cried since the day my aunt had a heart attack and we were going to be sent to the orphanage. There was an extremely tall Norfolk pine tree in our neighbor's yard. I climbed to its top many times, looking toward Sand Island. I was able to make out the approximate area of Sand Island near Aloha Tower.

One night, in the middle of a thunderstorm, I climbed the tree again to the very top. As I huddled there in the rain, I heard a brand new song by Bing Crosby from somebody's loud radio—*I'm Dreaming of a White Christmas*. The words triggered tears and I cried and cried. I missed my parents so much. Since then, every Christmas when I hear that song, for a short time I am transported back to that stormy night. Painful memories invade my conscious thoughts, but I quickly snatch myself back to the present.

Besides the alcoholic living in our house, my mother had always suspected another client as an informer. According to his transferred records from other facilities, he was known as a hopeless troublemaker. He had a glass eye and a stiff leg. Mom had reprimanded him for harassing one of the nurses.

One day, as I was standing in the living room of our home, I happened to glance out a window. A car was slowly, slowly rolling by. The same man with the glass eye was in it. We made eye contact. Like a bolt of lightning, fear streaked through me and I dropped to the floor. I was terrified. How did he know where we lived? Would he report us? Would the three of us now be forced apart and sent to an orphanage?

For days I waited for the men in suits and hats to make an appearance. When no one showed up after two weeks, I felt a little better again. However, he knew where we were, and I never felt safe. I was always in fear of separation and very much on the alert for anyone who looked suspicious or asked questions.

Mr. Reed, who was also handling other properties for my parents, did not give us a cent. He was pocketing the rent money while the bills were piling up. Mr. Reed never gave an accounting to anyone. Due to a lack of funds (or so Reed said), he sold off a beautiful piece of our Manoa Valley property and kept a large amount of the money. We found out later that the rest of it was used to pay off a mortgage.

Mom had asked the officers of various savings & loans if they could please manage the rest of the properties. At first they appeared helpful, but after talking to Mr. Reed, they declined. One officer with an attitude of patriotic fervor was quite nasty. In response to my mother's letter, the Secretary of the Federal Savings and Loan wrote:

> You asked if there is any law in the Territory of Hawaii or Federal Statute that gives American citizens protection if detained. This territory is under *martial law* that supersedes all other laws in times like these. In my opinion, Uncle Sam isn't going to room and board a person at his expense unless he has a mighty good reason to do so and your being held in detention, apparently, looks as though it was no one's fault but your own, and there is nothing that can be done about it but to take your own medicine.

You can imagine my mother's despair, a U.S. citizen and innocent! But this was the common attitude that we faced for many years after World War II. It was obvious that Mr. Reed was lying and painting my parents as Nazi sympathizers for his own greed. Perhaps he was one of the despicable informers. It certainly looked that way, and his reward was to have power of attorney over my parents' property in exchange for false information.

On June 21, 1943, Mom was released on parole. The next day she went down to Territorial Savings and Loan and just barely prevented the sale of another property. Mr. Reed had hardly paid anything on the mortgage and the property was about to be repossessed and sold.

After Dad's release, we left our rented Waikiki house and moved near Diamondhead, into one of our own homes that Mom had managed to save. Fortunately, it had just become vacant. The money from the other rentals began to trickle in and our business once again got started from scratch.

All of us worked hard. My older sister and I did the housekeeping, cooking, and clean-up chores. Dad took a job as supervisor of maintenance in the Coca-Cola plant in Honolulu, but he was fired after six months. It was brought to the attention of management that Dad had not only been detained, which they knew, but that he was (as told to them) "a very dangerous spy." He was also advised that they were afraid he could put poison into the Coke bottles and thereby poison hundreds of military troops.

Martial law ended on October 24, 1944, but that wasn't the end of our family's unhappy journey. The torment scarred our psyches in ways that would haunt us for the rest of our lives. But Mom and Dad didn't just give up and go under. The internment caused the breakup of many families. However, Dad and Mom loved each other as dearly as if they were teenage sweethearts. I believe their strength came from the support they gave one another. It seemed that adversity made them stronger. Both of them did a superb job of keeping the family together. Their philosophy was, "Bad things happen in life, but that is no reason to give up. Only cowards give up, so pick up your bootstraps, move forward, and achieve."

FOURTEEN

AFTERMATH

The arrest and internment of enemy aliens had two basic purposes. According to government files, the primary purpose was to exchange internees for the thousands of American businessmen, diplomats, students, tourists, and prisoners of war trapped in Nazi Germany. The secondary reason was to round up the most dangerous elements in American society.

The exchange program began in May 1942 with a series of diplomatic notes between Washington and Berlin spelling out what each side could expect from the other. The notes established security arrangements, identifying marks to be painted on the sides of the ships, how many suitcases each person was allowed, and a list of items they could and could not take with them. Even though the German government agreed to the terms, they often failed to keep their promises.

Internees to be exchanged for Americans were held in the camps until space became available on the *S.S. Drotingholm* and the *S.S. Gripsholm*.[1] When additional space was required, prisoners were loaded aboard *Acadia, Nyassa, Serpa Pinto,* and other ships. The U.S. government divided everyone into four categories: German diplomatic personnel, internees from Latin America, enemy aliens in American internment camps, and Germans who were not in camps but under surveillance by the FBI. On more than one occasion, the U.S. State Department offered to repatriate every German alien in the United States if Berlin would do the same with every American trapped in Nazi Germany.

The Special War Problems Office of the State Department was set up to operate a small number of internment facilities for diplomats and their families from the Axis countries. The "Special War Problems" included diplomats and consular corps staff and their families, as well as executives of Axis-owned businesses located in the U.S. and Latin America.

International protocol required above-average treatment for diplomats and their dependents while awaiting repatriation. Unlike the internees relegated to camps, diplomats, businessmen, and their families were housed in hotels and resorts. The State Department reported that 785 people were interned in hotels. Additional diplomats and their families were later interned in 1943. One witness described the treatment afforded them as provided in "a regal manner."[2]

Assembly Inn, Montreat, North Carolina. From October 29, 1942, to April 30, 1943, the Assembly Inn was home to 138 Japanese wives and children of diplomats and 130 German diplomats, wives, and children. The German contingent was housed on the two lower floors while the Japanese women and children were primarily on the upper third floor. Representatives from the State Department and Department of Justice were on duty twenty-four hours a day.

Homestead Hotel, Hot Springs, Virginia. December 19, 1941, to April 4, 1942, 159 German, Italian, Hungarian, and Bulgarian diplomats and their families, plus 335 Japanese diplomats and their families, all from embassies in Washington, DC, were housed at the Homestead Hotel.

Greenbrier Hotel, White Sulphur Springs, West Virginia. December 19, 1941, to June 1942, the Greenbrier hosted a variety of diplomats and their families from Axis countries, including the Japanese from the Homestead Hotel. In its seven months as a diplomatic confinement facility, the hotel housed up to 852 detainees.

Other hotels included the Ingleside Hotel in Staunton, Virginia, the Cascade Inn in Hot Springs, Virginia, the Shenvalee Hotel in New Market, Virginia, the Bedford Springs Hotel in Bedford Springs, Pennsylvania, and the Grove Park Inn in Asheville, North

Carolina. On February 14, 1944, the State Department shut down the Diplomatic Confinement Program.

Once the diplomats were exchanged, Washington turned its attention to the German citizens from Latin America, and finally to the internees in the INS detention camps. The State Department was more than willing to provide free one-way trips to Germany for anyone who wanted to go.

The government placed ads in newspapers across the country, addressed to the enemy alien population at large, offering to return them to their homeland. The ads were ineffective, and there were few takers. The State Department even sent telegrams to German citizens in the New York metropolitan area, offering them space on the *Drottningholm* for a free trip to Germany. Only twenty-two Germans in the New York area accepted the offer.

Despite the horrendous conditions of wartime Germany, a large number of internees took advantage of the government offer. Of the 634 prisoners from Crystal City who were repatriated to Germany, 357 were from Latin America. The story was much the same at the other camps as well. Internees stepped forward and volunteered to be returned to Germany.

Though many of them had never visited Germany or even remembered it, the internees wanted to leave the United States for a variety of reasons. Some were bitter at the outrageous treatment they received at the hands of the government. Some had rediscovered their German roots and wanted to return to their ancestral home. Others were threatened with deportation if they refused to volunteer. This action would have prevented them from returning to the United States at some future date. In most cases, when an internee was selected for the exchange program, his family volunteered to go with him.

Prior to the January 1945 repatriation voyage of the *Gripsholm*, the State Department issued a memorandum entitled *A List of Articles Which May or May Not Be Taken Out of the United States by German Repatriates*. The list included furniture, garden tools, electrical appliances, radios, gold, books, personal artwork, and binoculars. Birth certificates and passports were the only documents the repatriates were allowed to take.

To facilitate shipboard storage and for ease of baggage inspection, the authorities wanted trunks that were uniform in construction and size. Carpenters in Crystal City and other camps constructed them of heavy lumber. Repatriated families were allowed one large trunk for each family member. The contents included newly purchased items from mail order catalogs, clothing that was knitted or sewn by the wives, blankets, jackets, overcoats, and handmade jewelry boxes with intricate inlaid designs. Since none of the families had any jewelry anyway, once they arrived in Germany they might have intended to trade the contents of the boxes for food or other items.[3]

The irony of collecting and packing all their belongings in trunks was that upon arrival in Bregenz, Austria, it would be impossible to transport the trunks on to their final destination. Because train service was sporadic at best, all available space was reserved for the transport of troops and war material. The trunks were stored in a large warehouse for forwarding when transport was available and were never seen again. According to officials of the Austrian government, the warehouse was looted by French occupation troops stationed in that section of postwar Austria. Once again, the repatriates lost everything but the clothes on their backs.[4]

The story of the Eiserloh family is typical of what many families suffered during the forced repatriation. The war in Europe was still raging in January 1945 when Mathias and Johanna Eiserloh and their three American-born children were loaded aboard the *Gripsholm* for the long voyage across the Atlantic. They were herded into boxcars for the trip to Bregenz, and upon arrival in the city were exchanged for American prisoners. From Bregenz, the family traveled north to Frankfurt, sometimes on foot and sometimes on a troop train. It was on the train from Frankfurt to Johanna's hometown of Idstien/Taunus that they were strafed by eight P-38 American fighter planes.[5]

Starving, half frozen, and wearing bedraggled clothes, the Eiserlohs were forced to live in the cramped basement of a relative's home. Since they had come from America, the neighbors ridiculed them and viewed them with hostility and suspicion. The Gestapo suspected Mathias of being a spy for the advancing American army. He was questioned, beaten severely in front of his family by six men from Hitler's SS, and dragged away to a prison camp. Months later, he was freed and reunited with his family when U.S. troops overran the camp and freed the prisoners.

Transporting hundreds of prisoners from the camps to the *Gripsholm* created a logistical nightmare for the authorities. Every thirty minutes, trains loaded with German nationals and Canadian POWs pulled into the Exchange Place Station in Jersey City. Under heavy guard, they boarded buses for the trip from the train station to Pier F. The internees from Ellis Island were transported to the pier by Coast Guard cutter.

The special train bearing the prisoners from Fort Lincoln, North Dakota, was due to arrive on January 6 but was delayed for one day by sub-zero weather and three different train wrecks along the route of travel.[6]

The Canadian Hospital Ship *Letetia* arrived in New York Harbor on the afternoon of January 6. It was originally intended for the ship to proceed up the Hudson River to Camp Shanks to load her passengers. With the bad weather and the large ice floes impeding further travel upriver, the *Letetia* was diverted to the White Star Cunard Pier 90 in New York City.

The *Gripsholm's* manifest listed 1,045 German repatriates on board. This number included 754 German civilians from the United States, 102 German civilians from Mexico, 186 POWs from the United States, and 21 German POWs from Canada. Passengers aboard the *Letetia* included 400 German nationals and 547 German POWs.

The staterooms were not much bigger than a large closet. Families piled their luggage anywhere they could find room. As soon as they were settled into their new quarters, they worked their way along narrow passageways in an effort to find their friends or to go up on deck for fresh air.

The *Gripsholm* sailed on January 7, 1945, followed a few hours later by the *Letetia*. Passengers stood on deck to watch the New York skyline and the Statue of Liberty disappear into the distance. They were leaving a country that had imprisoned them and now were being forced to journey to a war-ravaged country that many of them had never seen.

For three weeks they crossed the Atlantic to Marseille. The children thought it was a great adventure while the parents lived in terror of the U-boats and what awaited them when they reached their new home. Remembering this voyage in later years, many of the internees said that the Swedish sailors were polite and the food was excellent.

The war in Europe ended in May 1945, but the deportation of enemy aliens continued. On July 14, 1945, President Harry S. Truman signed Proclamation 2655 into law. It stated in part:

> All alien enemies now or hereafter interned within the continental limits of the United States pursuant to the proclamations of the President of the United States who shall be deemed by the Attorney General to be dangerous to the public peace and safety of the United States because they adhered to the aforesaid enemy governments or the principals of government thereof shall be subject under the order of the Attorney General to removal from the United States and may be required to depart therefrom in accordance with such regulations as he may prescribe.[7]

Two months later, the Inter-American Conference on Problems of War and Peace met in Mexico City. Resolution VII was adopted, recommending the implementation of measures to prevent any person whose deportation should be deemed necessary for reasons of security of the continent from further residing in that hemisphere, if such residence was prejudicial to the future security or welfare of the Americas. The governments of Latin America had sent a clear message. The kidnapped aliens were Washington's problem and they didn't want them back.

Under the auspices of the Inter-American Conference and pursuant to the Alien Enemy Act of 1798, Truman signed Proclamation 2662 to include all kidnapped enemy aliens from Latin America in the repatriation program. It was later superseded by Proclamation 2685, which declared:

> All alien enemies within the continental limits of the United States brought here from other American Republics after December 7, 1941, who are within the territory of the United States without admission under the immigration laws, shall, if their continued residence in the Western Hemisphere is deemed by the Secretary of State to be prejudicial to the future security or welfare of the Americas, be subject upon order of the Secretary of State to removal from the United States and may be required to depart

therefrom in accordance with such regulations as the Secretary of State may prescribe.[8]

Truman decided that once an internee received his deportation notice, thirty days was a reasonable amount of time to affect the recovery, disposal, and removal of his goods and effects and to prepare for his departure. When the head of the family was selected for deportation, wives and children were permitted to join him.

One of the first Germans to be deported was Fritz Kuhn, self-styled "American Fuhrer" and leader of the American Bund. On September 10, 1945, Kuhn and a group of forty-nine German nationals were escorted up the gangway of the *Antioch Victory*. Once the ship was underway, Auxiliary Foreign Service Officer Floyd J. Dubas was responsible for the transportation and delivery of the prisoners to the United States military authorities at Bremen, Germany.[9]

Prior to their departure from New York, a representative of the Immigration and Naturalization Service gave Dubas a list in duplicate showing the amount and types of currency in the possession of each deportee. He was also given property envelopes belonging to the repatriates. These contained traveler's checks in amounts exceeding the sixty-dollar maximum that each deportee carried.

The list and the envelopes were to be turned over to military authorities upon arrival in Bremen. The military was responsible for taking custody of the checks and converting them into local currency. They were also responsible for the money the deportees carried on their persons.

Before the *Antioch Victory* reached its destination, Dubas received a list of the deportees so he could check the passengers as they disembarked. He was ordered to personally turn Kuhn over to the authorities. Once his task was complete, Dubas was given a receipt for the deportees and the property envelopes.

In addition to the Eiserlohs, other families suffered harsh treatment at the hands of the U.S. military. After the war ended, Lambert and Paula Jacobs and their two sons were repatriated from Ellis Island aboard the *Aiken Victory* on January 17, 1946. When the Jacobs family disembarked in occupied Germany, armed U.S. soldiers, who called the family "American Nazis," surrounded them and escorted them to waiting railroad cars. For the entire trip across Germany, they were locked inside dark, unheated cattle cars with nothing to sustain them but bread and water.

Art Jacobs celebrated his thirteenth birthday alone in a prison cell in Hohenasperg. His neighbors were high-ranking German officers suspected of Nazi war crimes and German civilians who were being denazified.

> For almost four decades I questioned my memory about the hangman's tree. I repeatedly asked myself, "Was there really a hangman's tree in that place?" Did I dream it? Were there bullet marks on the hangman's tree? Did I also imagine those other horrible things? Any time I was out of my cell I was under the watchful eyes of armed guards. Did I dream that my armed guard shouted, "Do you see that big tree in the courtyard, it's the hangman tree?" "Make sure," the soldier said, "that you don't ever take your hands off the top of your head when you are out of your cell. The guards escorted me to and from my cell for each meal. I was required to eat in a standing position, with armed guards all around me, staring at me, whispering among themselves. I, the prisoner, was required to be silent. I was ever reminded by my guard not to talk to other prisoners while I was eating. He reminded me that I was to eat in silence; and when I was finished, to stand there with my hands on my head until I was ordered to move on. Several times, I blurted out, "Sir, I am an American!" The soldier snapped back, "Shut up, you Nazi! Remember what I told you about the hangman's tree." As usual, I became frightened and stood there speechless.[10]

With the release, parole, and exchange of the internees, the INS began to close down the internment camps and transfer the remaining prisoners to other camps. Camp Kenedy was shut down in September 1944. After the last internees were transferred out of Seagoville in June 1945, the facility became a minimum-security prison for men. Due to soaring crime rates and overcrowding, Seagoville is now a maximum-security prison.

Fort Lincoln, near Bismarck, North Dakota, ceased operations on March 1, 1946. It remained abandoned until June 1969 when Congress voted to provide funds for a Native-American training center.

Today, Fort Lincoln houses the United Tribes Technical College.

The former Civilian Conservation Corps (CCC) camp at Fort Stanton, New Mexico, was shut down on November 20, 1945. After five years of continued use, the portable, prefabricated barracks that hadn't been dismantled and shipped to other INS facilities were turned over to the Fort Stanton Hospital.

As the camps were emptied of their inhabitants, the remaining internees were transferred to the last operational internment facility at Crystal City. These internees were required to dismantle the buildings on the Japanese side of the camp. The prefabricated victory huts were packed up and shipped to Border Patrol stations and other federal facilities. Camp Crystal City officially closed its gates in February 1948, and the last internees were sent home or shipped to Ellis Island for further disposition.

With the surrender of the German military, hostilities between America and Germany ended in May 1945. However, it wasn't until October 19, 1951, that both houses of Congress passed a resolution terminating the state of war that had existed between the United States and Germany since December 11, 1941. "Resolved by the Senate and House of Representatives of the United States of America in Congress assembled, that the state of war declared to exist between the United States and the government of Germany by the joint resolution of Congress approved December 11, 1941, is hereby terminated and such termination shall take effect on the date of the enactment of this resolution."[11]

None of the internees arrested on the mainland or in Hawaii, or those brought to the United States from Latin America were ever charged with anything, including sabotage, espionage, or subversion. Their only crime was to have been born of the same ethnicity as citizens of the Axis powers. For more than sixty years, the United States government has refused to acknowledge its part in this shameful episode. Likewise, historians, politicians, and educators still insist that Germans and Italians were never interned, despite an abundance of evidence in the form of FBI and State Department memos and documents, as well as eyewitness accounts.

On August 6, 1946, 700 enemy aliens on Ellis Island, including 305 Germans, faced imminent deportation as a result of a decision by the United States Circuit Court of Appeals. The court upheld a prior ruling by District Judge Simon H. Rifkind in which he dismissed a writ of habeas corpus in a test case involving Herman Schlueter, an eighty-one-year-old bartender and a member of the German American Bund.[12]

During the trial, Schlueter protested that he wasn't permitted an attorney or the privilege of examining witnesses. Judge Rifkind stated that in his opinion, Schlueter wasn't even entitled to a hearing and therefore couldn't complain about the quality of the hearing he received.

As soon as the circuit court announced its decision, Assistant United States Attorney Stanley Lowell announced that the Department of Justice planned to proceed with the deportation of the three hundred Germans as quickly as possible, along with the four hundred Japanese citizens interned on the West Coast. Lowell further stated that the decision of the circuit court also applied to several hundred enemy aliens from Latin America. He indicated that no action would be taken to deport them until the circuit court had ruled on a decision by District Judge Robert R. Nevin in the case of Hans von Heymann, a former resident of Costa Rica. In that case, Judge Nevin ruled that it made no difference whether an enemy alien was brought to the United States involuntarily, because political and diplomatic policies were not subject to judicial review.

The court's decision sustained the constitutionality of the Enemy Alien Act of 1798 and that the U.S. Attorney General was correct in not granting a due process hearing to enemy aliens. The proclamations issued by the President of the United States calling for the seizure of said enemy aliens were also deemed constitutionally correct. The ruling further stipulated that the Enemy Alien Act of 1798 was still in operation despite the cessation of hostilities.

In the case of Herman Schleuter, the court issued the following ruling: "We agree with Judge Rifkind that the law authorized the making of an order of deportation of an enemy alien without a court order and without a hearing of any kind. Court jurisdiction arises only when a complaint is filed by a citizen. When the procedure is through executive action, the statute calls for no hearing in court or elsewhere."[13]

"The action of the Attorney General in denying a due process hearing is based on a construction of the Enemy Alien Act by Justice Washington in a case arising in 1817, when it was held that Presidential proclamation in time of war was sufficient authority for this procedure in the cases of alien enemies deemed to be dangerous to the public safety and peace."[14]

Even though Germany surrendered in May 1945, the last enemy aliens were not released until July 1948, more than three years after hostilities ended. On May 18, 1948, Commissioner of Immigration Watson B. Miller led reporters from various news agencies on a tour of the detention facilities on Ellis Island. In a statement to reporters he said, "I am in favor of a more modern and better arranged system for detaining aliens."[15]

Wherever the reporters ventured on the island—in the cafeteria, dormitories, and recreation hall—the aliens bombarded them with notes, petitions, and statements of their loyalty to America. Other internees tried to tell their stories whenever they could corner a reporter for even a few minutes. Most of the complaints came from among the 169 Germans who were held on the island as enemy aliens on and off since the start of World War II. According to the reporters, all of the Germans said they were loyal Americans. Many stated that their wives and families were born in this country and that their sons had fought in the United States Army.

In the cafeteria, the detainees and the reporters sat down for a lunch of soup, liver, boiled potatoes, french-fried turnips, Jell-O, rice, coffee, and bread. They ate from tin trays but were not allowed to have knives. Chief of Detention, Deportation, and Parole Philip Forman was also present at the meal and stated that the government spent a dollar and five cents on food for each person each day.

Many of the internees seldom ate in the mess hall but lived primarily on food sent in from relatives on the outside or supplies they purchased in the canteen run by German inmates. Coffee sold for three cents a cup, milk for six cents, and bacon and two eggs for twenty-two cents.

On a trip back from Ellis Island, Miller told his guest:

> The Enemy Alien Act of 1798, under which the Germans
> are being held and which gives the President power to use them

in any way he sees fit during wartime, is now being contested in court. In addition to the Germans, there are on the island 215 persons awaiting deportation, none of them listed as subversive, incidentally, 117 applying for admission including a number of stowaways and 78 miscellaneous aliens. Under peak conditions the island can house 2000.[16]

One of the more ominous aspects of the repatriation program was the apparent internment and repatriation of German Jews from Latin America. Official documents and other evidence reveal that the United States government was interning German Jews and shipping them to Nazi Germany as part of the exchange program.

In his article "German Jews Interned in the United States," Arthur Jacobs wrote:

When I first started my research of the internment of German Americans in the United States during World War II, I interviewed several former internees independently of one another who were adults during the time of their internment, unlike myself who was only twelve back then. During one or more of these interviews, the subject of the German American and the German Latin American internees who were Jewish was mentioned by the interviewee.

One former internee described to me that a group of Panamanians who were German Jews were interned with him in Camp Forrest, Tennessee. During this interview he described, even though the German Jews from Panama were placed in a separate compound, the only separation was a barbed-wire fence. He recalled how he and other internees visited with a group from Panama by chatting through the fence. In addition, during the evening hours, many of the German internees from the United States would slip through the fencing and visit with the Panamanian group in their huts.[17]

On November 30, 1994, and again on September 4, 1998, *Dateline NBC* aired a program entitled *Roundup*. In this program, it was noted that German Jews were aboard an exchange vessel and among a group of civilian internees who were to be exchanged for Americans held captive in Nazi Germany. Prior to *Dateline's* broadcast, Arthur Jacobs came across the following passage: "Passing the heavily guarded compound containing German and Japanese prisoners of war (POWs), Rabbi Isreal Gerstein of Chattanooga, Tennessee, arrived at the room where the Jews were kept. It was a moving experience—it was a Tisha B'Av mood. This was not North Africa or liberated Europe—it was Fort Oglethorpe, Georgia."[18]

When President Roosevelt signed Executive Order 9066, he authorized the exclusion of 120,000 Japanese Americans and legal resident aliens from the West Coast of the United States, as well as the internment of United States citizens and legal permanent residents of Japanese ancestry. The freedom of German Americans and Italian Americans was also restricted by measures that branded them enemy aliens and implemented the use of identification cards, travel restrictions, seizure of personal property, and internment.

Over the years, the government has recognized the injustices that were perpetrated against the Japanese and the Italians, but for the Germans, nothing. Thirty-four years to the day after Roosevelt signed the now infamous order, President Gerald Ford formally rescinded Executive Order 9066. In the proclamation repealing the order, Ford said: "I call upon the American People to affirm with me this American Promise, that we have learned from the tragedy of that long ago experience forever to treasure liberty and justice for each individual American, and to resolve that this kind of action shall never again be repeated."[19]

On July 31, 1980, President Jimmy Carter signed legislation establishing the Commission on Wartime Relocation and Internment of Civilians to investigate the claim that the incarceration of Japanese Americans and legal resident aliens during World War II was justified by military necessity. The commission held twenty days of hearings and heard testimony from 750 witnesses. In its final report, *Personal Justice Denied*, the commission concluded that the promulgation of Executive Order 9066 was not justified by military necessity, and that the decision to issue the order was shaped by "race prejudice, war hysteria, and a failure of political leadership."

Twelve years later, the Japanese received their apology and restitution from the government when Congress passed and President Reagan signed the Civil Liberty Act of 1988. The Act formally acknowledged and apologized for "fundamental violations of the basic civil liberties and constitutional rights of individuals of Japanese ancestry." In a public signing ceremony, President Reagan quoted his own words honoring Japanese American soldiers and all American soldiers who fought in World War II. "Blood that has soaked into the sands of a beach is all of one color. America stands unique in the world, the only country not founded on race but on a way, an ideal. Not in spite of, but because of our polyglot background, we have had all the strength in the world. That is the American way. Here we admit a wrong. Here we affirm our commitment as a Nation to equal justice under the law."[20]

The Italians also suffered under the provisions of Executive Order 9066. Like the Germans and the Japanese, they were subjected to the use of identification cards, travel restrictions, and seizure of personal property. According to the findings of Congress in writing the Wartime Violation of Italian American Civil Liberties Act, the freedom of more than six hundred thousand Italian-born immigrants and their families was restricted by government measures that branded them "enemy aliens." Congress also discovered that thousands of Italian American immigrants were arrested during World War II and of that number, hundreds were interned in military camps.

In writing the act, Congress recognized the hundreds of thousands of Italian Americans who performed exemplary service and the thousands who sacrificed their lives in defense of the United States. Congress also acknowledged that the impact of the wartime experience was devastating to Italian American communities in the United States and that its effects were still being felt more than fifty years later.

Last, Congress wrote, "A deliberate government policy kept these measures from the public during the war. Even fifty years later, much information is still classified, the full story remains unknown to the public, and it has never been acknowledged in any official capacity by the United States Government."[21]

The Italians were recognized when the 106th Congress adopted the Wartime Violation of Italian American Civil Liberties Act. President Clinton signed the act into law on November 7, 2000.

The act required the Attorney General to conduct a comprehensive review of the treatment Italian Americans received at the hands of the U.S. government and list the names of those who were arrested and interned along with the locations where they were interned. Other provisions of the act required the FBI to provide documentation of the raids on the homes of Italian Americans, a list of ports they were restricted from, and the names of those individuals prevented from pursuing their livelihood in prohibited areas. The Attorney General was also directed to provide the names of individuals whose boats were confiscated by the FBI and any Italian American railroad workers who were prevented from working in the prohibited zones.

Pursuant to the act, Congress instructed the Attorney General to provide a list of all civil liberties infringements suffered by Italian Americans as a result of Executive Order 9066, including internment, hearings without benefit of counsel, illegal searches and seizures, travel restrictions, enemy alien registration requirements, employment restrictions, confiscation of property, and forced evacuation from their homes.

Fifty-six years after the end of World War II, Senator Russell Feingold and Charles Grassley introduced the Wartime Treatment Study Act on the floor of the Senate. Shortly thereafter, Representative Robert Wexler introduced the legislation in the House. That act would simply create commissions to study the wartime treatment of European Americans and Latin Americans, as well as the denial of asylum by the United States to Jews fleeing persecution in Germany. With respect to the American Commission, the bill requires the development of a list of internees, camps, and exchange voyages, as well as an analysis of the facts, circumstances and underlying rationale for the related government policies.

Since August 2001, the Wartime Treatment Study Act has been reintroduced to both houses of Congress four times, each time with similar results. On March 10, 2009, Senator Feingold and Congressman Wexler reintroduced the bill to their respective houses of Congress. Section 2, Findings of the Wartime Treatment Study Act states:

> During World War II, the United States Government arrested, interned, or otherwise detained thousands of European Americans, some remaining in custody for years after cessation of

World War II hostilities, and repatriated, exchanged, or deported European Americans, including American-born children, to European Axis nations to be exchanged for Americans held in those nations.

Pursuant to a policy coordinated by the United States with Latin American nations, many Latin Americans, including German and Austrian Jews, were arrested, relocated to the United States, and interned. Many were later repatriated or deported to European Axis nations during World War II and exchanged for Americans and Latin Americans held in those nations.

Millions of European Americans served in the Armed Forces and thousands sacrificed their lives in defense of the United States.

Time is of the essence for the establishment of commissions, because of the increasing danger of destruction and loss of relevant documents, the advanced age of potential witnesses and, most importantly, the advanced age of those affected by the United States Government's policies. Many who suffered have already passed away and will never know of this effort.[22]

If passed, the act would require the European American Commission to review the facts and circumstances surrounding the United States government's actions during World War II with respect to European Americans and European Latin Americans pursuant to the Alien Enemies Act; Presidential Proclamations 2526, 2527, 2655, 2662, and 2685; Executive Orders 9066 and 9055; and any directive of the United States government pursuant to such laws, proclamations, or executive orders respecting the registration, arrest, exclusion, internment, exchange, or deportation of European Americans and European Latin Americans.

The Commission would also assess the underlying rationale of the United States government's decision to develop related programs and policies, the information the United States government received or acquired suggesting the related programs and policies were necessary, and the perceived benefit of enacting such programs and policies on European Americans and European Latin Americans and their communities.

The Commission would review laws, proclamations, and executive orders relating to registration requirements, travel and property restrictions, establishment of restricted areas, raids, arrests, internment, and exclusion policies relating to the families and property that excludees and internees were forced to abandon, as well as exchange, repatriation, and deportation, and the immediate and long-term effects of such actions, particularly internment, on the lives of those affected.

The Wartime Treatment Study Act contains a comprehensive list of specific actions the Commissioners would be required to take in implementing the act, including compilation of a list of all temporary and long-term internment facilities in the United States and Latin America, the names of internees who died while in the detention facilities and where they were buried, the names of children of internees and where they were born, a list of the nations from which European Latin Americans were brought to the United States, locations where internees were exchanged for persons held in European Axis nations, ships that transported them to Europe, and all respective departure and disembarkation ports.

The Wartime Treatment Study Act of 2009 was referred to the Committee on the Judiciary for further action. On March 13, 2009, The Subcommittee on Immigration, Citizenship, Refugees, Border Security, and International Law held a series of hearings and heard testimony from a number of witnesses. At the present time, the Wartime Treatment Study Act is awaiting further action from both the Senate and the House of Representatives.

In the interest of national security, during World War II, the U.S. Government concealed the specific details of the internment camps and the hostage exchange program from the American public. Guards at the camps were required to sign statements agreeing not to reveal information about the camps. The internees were also warned not to talk and maintained their silence for the rest of their lives. They lived in fear that the FBI would once again come knocking on their doors.

Many internees have kept their stories hidden from their families and the world. Many of them felt shame and fear long after the war ended. Even after more than six decades of silence, they will not talk to researchers or allow their real names to be used in books and articles. The people who were forced to endure these injustices are dying. Unless action is taken to preserve their memories of that terrible time, their stories will be lost forever.

In his closing remarks on the Wartime Treatment Study Act, Senator Russell Feingold said:

> It is so urgent that we pass this legislation. We cannot wait any longer. The injustices to European Americans and Jewish refugees occurred more than 50 years ago. The people who were affected by these policies are dying. Americans must learn from these tragedies now, before there is no one left. We cannot put this off any longer. These people have suffered long enough without official independent study of what happened to them and without knowing this Nation recognizes their sacrifice and resolves to learn from the mistakes of the past that caused them so much pain.[23]

The Wartime Treatment Study Act was attached to the Immigration Reform Bill of 2009, and for the fifth time it failed to become law.

NOTES

1. Mercy Voyages of the MS *Drottingholm* and MS *Gripsholm*, Swedish American Lines, Gothenburg, Sweden.
2. "World War II Detention of Diplomats and Families," *Montreat History Spotlight*, 2008.
3. Email, Eberhard Fuhr, March 31, 2009.
4. Ibid.
5. Lothar Eiserloh, "The Eiserloh Family Story."
6. Departure of Exchange Vessel M.S. *Gripsholm* and Canadian Hospital Ship *Letetia,* Doc. 100, Department of State, January 10, 1945.
7. Presidential Proclamation 2655, Removal of Alien Enemies, July 14, 1945.
8. Presidential Proclamation 2685, Removal of Alien Enemies, April 10, 1946.
9. Alfred Khun, 2, M13/Final Disposition, *Freedom of Information Times,* September 10, 1945.
10. Arthur Jacobs, *The Prison Called Hohenasperg* (Boca Raton, Florida: Universal Publishing Company, 1999).
11. Joint Resolution to Congress to Terminate the State of War Between the United States and Germany, 65 Stat. 451, October 19, 1951.
12. "700 Enemy Aliens Facing Ouster at Early date Under New Ruling,"

New York Times (1923), Jan. 3, 1947 (ProQuest Historical Newspapers: *The New York Times* [1851–2007]).

13. United States ex. Rel. Schleuter vs. Watkins as Director of Immigration and Naturalization, U.S. District Court for the Southern district of New York, 67F. Supp. 556; U.S. District Lexis 2198, August 6, 1941.

14. "200 Enemy Aliens Held on Ellis Island, New York," *New York Times*, September 11, 1947.

15. "700 Enemy Aliens Facing Ouster at Early Date," *New York Times*, January 3, 1947.

16. Watson B. Miller, Commissioner, News Conference, May 18, 1948.

17. Arthur Jacobs, "Jews Interned in the United States," *Freedom of Information Times*, March 23, 2009.

18. Harvey Strum, "Jewish Internees in the American South, 1942–1945," American Jewish Archives, Spring 1990, No. 1, p. 27.

19. In 1976, President Ford formally rescinded Executive Order 9066.

20. President Reagan signed the Civil Liberties Act of 1988, formally acknowledging and apologizing for elimination of basic civil liberties and Constitutional rights of individuals of Japanese ancestry.

21. In 2000, President Clinton signed the Wartime Violation of Italian American Civil Liberties Act.

22. Wartime Treatment Study Act, HR 1425, 110th Congress, March 19, 2009.

23. Remarks of U.S. Senator Feingold on the Wartime Treatment Study Act Amendment to the Comprehensive Immigration Reform Act, May 24, 2007.

FIFTEEN

THE EISERLOH FAMILY

Lothar Eiserloh

Mathias and Johanna Eiserloh met in Johanna's hometown of Idstein, Germany, after World War I, where Mathias was a civil engineering student. They shared a dream of immigrating to America and did so in 1922. Mathias and Johanna brought with them the hopes and dreams held by most immigrants to this country—to live, work, and raise a family in freedom. Mathias's two sisters and three of Johanna's siblings joined them in America soon after.

Life was not as rosy in America as they had imagined. Mathias and Johanna endured the struggles typically faced by new immigrants while learning the new language, finding employment, and adjusting to cultural and social differences. During those early years, the two of them accepted jobs wherever they could find work. Mathias even worked briefly in the coal mines of West Virginia. Eventually, he found a job in his chosen profession. In 1929, they rewarded themselves by vacationing in Europe, traveling, and visiting family.

In October, days before their return, the stock market crashed. Mathias and Johanna came home to face financial turmoil and the Great Depression. Eventually, after struggling to recoup their losses, they purchased two acres of land in a rural area outside Cleveland, Ohio. Mathias, who had also studied architecture, designed and drew plans for a home, which the couple literally built with their own hands while living in a tent on the property. With the help of friends, they dug the basement, mixed and poured cement for the foundation, and built a fine house. They bore three children between 1930 and 1941—all U.S. citizens.

During this time, Johanna also raised a flock of chickens and started a small business selling eggs and hens. Life was good, the future looked bright, and the children flourished. The Eiserlohs attended a German social club largely comprised of other engineers and their families with whom they enjoyed German music and dances and shared common experiences. Such clubs also served as networks for finding jobs and giving support to members in times of need. While the men would discuss their jobs and politics over a stein of beer and a cigarette, this club was strictly social. It was not a political organization nor did it have a political agenda.

Busy raising their children and working hard, the Eiserlohs, unlike their siblings, had not yet pursued their long-standing plan to apply for U.S. citizenship. Naively, they had considered themselves thoroughly American since their arrival in this country. They were to learn quickly that this mistake and, apparently, their club member- ship would cost them everything.

Days after the attack on Pearl Harbor, on December 9, 1941, life as the Eiserlohs had known it was destroyed forever. Mathias was suddenly arrested by the FBI at his job and jailed in Cleveland. Their savings account was frozen. Mathias was questioned about his membership in the German club, their families here and in Europe, his friends, and his job. The government ordered his internment.

In desperation, Johanna was forced to sell their home after a few months. Fearing the proceeds from the sale would be frozen, Johanna insisted on a cash sale and found it necessary to accept the paltry sum offered by an opportunistic buyer. Before she could move out, a masked intruder attacked her during the night, demanding "the money." She fought him off with a piece of lead pipe, which she kept under her pillow for protection. Just days earlier, Johanna was unnerved because someone shot their two German Shepherds. Terri- fied and badly shaken, she was left partially paralyzed.

Mathias's sister gave the family shelter in her cellar and took care of the children while Johanna slowly recovered. A basement fire forced the family to find yet another home. The children were traumatized and missed their father terribly. Despite Johanna's many pleas, the government gave no indication when or if Mathias would be released. Reluctantly, Johanna petitioned the government to be allowed to join him in the camp, believing the family would be better off together.

After two long years of suffering the strain and hardship of separation, the family was reunited at the Crystal City, Texas, Internment Camp. Although Johanna and the children were "voluntary internees," they could not leave voluntarily. They lived in small quarters with very basic necessities. The Eiserlohs soon learned from other families in the camp that their story was not unique. Most had been suddenly uprooted and imprisoned, losing homes and possessions.

Becoming increasingly desperate and bitter, they finally agreed to repatriate to Germany in response to the more than subtle pressures by government officials. In January 1945, the Eiserlohs were transported to New York Harbor to board the *S.S. Gripsholm* under a wartime exchange program between Germany and the United States. The arrangement provided for U.S. citizens held in Germany to be released in exchange for Germans sent back from the United States. The Germans being exchanged included many children and spouses who were either U.S. born or naturalized citizens.

At age forty-four, Johanna was nine months pregnant when they left Crystal City. She gave birth to an infant son, Gunther, on January 4, 1945, on the train to New York Harbor and the *S.S. Gripsholm*. The child's birth certificate lists his place of birth as New Orleans, Louisiana. Although extremely weak from travel and the recent birth, Johanna had to board the *Gripsholm* with her family on January 6, 1945, and endure the fourteen-day stormy crossing through the Atlantic war zone. She and her baby, both weak and ill, remained in sickbay throughout the entire voyage. The older children were now fourteen, nine, and four years old.

Along with several hundred repatriates, the Eiserlohs disembarked from the *Gripsholm* at Marseilles, France, after a minor incident with a harbor mine. They were taken by train to Switzerland. While awaiting the exchange, the crates containing the family's belongings were stolen, including seasonal clothing carefully selected by Johanna and items they could barter for food. The family now had only the clothes they wore and one small suitcase of miscellaneous things.

The exchange took place at Bregenz in early February 1945. The Germans were brought to the border in small groups on the back of a flatbed truck. The Eiserlohs waited for hours in the cold until it was their turn to cross. Carrying the baby, Johanna walked with Ensila behind Mathias, Lothar, and Ingrid. Their papers were carefully checked and heads counted: two adults, two male children, two female children. The children, all U.S. citizens, were exchanged for other U.S. citizens who walked out to freedom. On the other side, the Eiserlohs climbed back onto the open truck and were taken to Aschaffenburg, a town almost completely destroyed by bombs.

Left on their own and struggling with the sickly infant, the Eiserlohs slowly made their way north across war-ravaged Germany. Amidst bombings and air raids, in the dead of a record-breaking winter, the family traveled by train whenever possible, but often had to walk because the railways were destroyed. Food was hard to come by, and they could only hope to find shelter among Johanna's relatives. The relatives were not expecting them because no communication had been possible since the start of the war.

During the last leg of the journey, U.S. planes strafed the train. Frightened, the Eiserlohs huddled under their seats until the train stopped. They ran into the adjoining woods as the planes continued gunning the train. An anti-aircraft gun on the last car was put into action, and the family watched with mixed emotions as smoke filled the sky where two of the American planes were shot down.

Hungry and exhausted from two months of difficult travel, the Eiserlohs arrived in Idstein during the first days of March. They were greeted without enthusiasm and felt most unwelcome. Like the rest of the country, Johanna's relatives did not have enough food for themselves, never mind another family of six. Her aging parents could only offer them a small corner in their cellar for living quarters. What little food could be had was primarily bartered on the black market. The family was by now suffering the symptoms of malnutrition. Having just arrived from America, they were often ill-treated and were under constant suspicion by the local Nazis and townspeople who could not comprehend why they had returned from America at this time.

Within two weeks of their arrival, six overzealous members of the SS severely beat Mathias in their basement home in full view of his terrified wife and children. The Gestapo arrested Mathias and took him away to an unknown prison, suspecting him of being an undercover spy for the advancing U.S. military. The family did not know if he was still alive until the end of the war some months later when he was found, thoroughly questioned, and released by the occupying U.S. Army. Ironically, the government that imprisoned him in America and was responsible for his family's predicament probably saved his life. Following the war, the Eiserlohs moved to a small two-room barracks facility. It was sparsely furnished, with beds in one room, and a table, four chairs, and a small coal stove in the other. It had a sink with cold running water in one corner, but no kitchen. From there, the family tried to rebuild their lives.

Their application for reentry to the U.S. immediately after the war was repeatedly denied. Finally, in 1947, the two eldest children, Ingrid and Lothar, then ages 12 and 17, were allowed to repatriate to the United States, with Mathias's sister agreeing to act as their guardian. They did not see their family again for eight years. The Eiserlohs continued to endure years of hunger and deprivation while making countless applications to reenter the United States. Lothar joined the Air Force after completing high school and was granted a security clearance to receive nuclear weapons training. Perhaps not coincidentally, his parents and siblings were finally granted reentry visas to the United States shortly thereafter in November 1955.

Now sixty years old, Mathias couldn't find work as a civil engineer. He accepted a low-paying job from which he was forced to retire at sixty-two. After struggling several more years to provide for his wife and two teenagers, he died of heart failure at age sixty-five. Johanna became a citizen in 1961 and supported herself with the meager earnings from odd jobs until the age of eighty-nine, when Alzheimer's robbed her of all her past memories. She died in January 1997 at the age of ninety-six.

Three children survive today. Gunther, who began his life on a train to New York, perished in an automobile accident at the age of twenty-two, after his discharge from the U.S. Navy. The physical, emotional, and psychological trauma the family suffered throughout the years of separation and deprivation had long-lasting effects on all of them and is still being felt by the remaining three children.

SIXTEEN

INJUSTICE REVISITED

Since World War I, America's wars have had a devastating effect on the civil liberties of its people. In the name of national security, the government has felt the need to take drastic action to protect its citizens from threats, perceived and real. These draconian measures have often violated the precepts of the Constitution and denied individuals and groups their due process and freedoms guaranteed by law. Eberhard Fuhr, whose story was highlighted earlier in this book, summed up this culture of fear when he said, "A sovereign nation has a duty to protect itself, but America's civil liberties should not be cast aside so freely, even in time of war."[1]

The events described in this book happened more than sixty years ago, but the parallels between the issues of the war years and the current political climate in the United States are startling. The oft-quoted adage "those who cannot remember the past are condemned to repeat it" rings true. Many of the questionable tactics imposed on citizens and non-citizens alike by the United Sates government in the last century are as prevalent today as they were in 1917.

Despite the obvious differences, the Black Tom explosion and the bombing of the World Trade Center bear an eerie resemblance to each other. Both of these attacks were carried out by foreign nationals and resulted in casualties and destruction in Lower Manhattan. They were a prelude to war and gave Congress the impetus to pass legislation that impacted all facets of American life. After the Black

Tom explosion, Congress passed the Espionage Acts of 1917 and the Sedition Act of 1918.[2] After the bombing of the World Trade Center, Congress passed the Patriot Act on October 25, 2001.[3]

No one was convicted of spying or sabotage under the Espionage Act during the war, but in the 1920s, federal prosecutors tried more than 2,000 cases, resulting in 1,055 convictions. Judges instructed juries that they could infer unlawful intent from the likely effects of a defendant's words. Judges also instructed juries that they could convict on the basis of bad tendency of the defendant's language whether or not prosecutors had proven their case.

Some judges tried to reconcile the act with free speech guaranteed by the First Amendment of the Constitution, but in three different cases, the U.S. Supreme Court upheld the constitutionality of the law and rejected all First Amendment challenges.

In many ways, the Patriot Act mirrors the Espionage Act and the Sedition Act. The title "USA Patriot Act" is an acronym for its stated purpose: Uniting and Strengthening of America by Providing Appropriate Tools Required to Intercept and Obstruct Terrorism. It was intended to deter and punish terrorist acts in the United States and around the world, to enhance law enforcement investigatory tools, and other purposes.

Appearing before the Department of Justice to announce the formation of the Foreign Terrorist Tracking Task Force on October 31, 2001, Attorney General Ashcroft said,

> The Department of Justice is moving forcefully to implement new authorities in our antiterrorism law. Today, the Immigration and Naturalization Service has issued guidance to immigration personnel, informing them about the new power that the Act provides for them in terms of the arrest, detention, and removal of terrorist aliens.
>
> The Act broadens the grounds of inadmissibility, that is grounds for which admission to the United States can be denied, to include representatives of groups that publicly endorse terrorist activity in the United States. It also makes aliens inadmissible if they provide material support to a designated terrorist organization; even if they don't specifically intend to support this terrorist activity, they are giving support to the organization that

conducts terrorist activities, and they can be denied admission to the United States. In most cases, aliens will be inadmissible under these new provisions for past support they have given to terrorist organizations.

In addition, the USA Patriot Act requires the detention of aliens whom the Attorney General certifies to be a threat to national security. If the Attorney General certifies that they are a threat to national security, they must be detained by a requirement of the USA Patriot Act, or if they are determined to have been engaged in terrorist activities. Once arrested, aliens must be charged within seven days under the Act. If charges are dismissed, the aliens will be released. Otherwise, charged aliens must be detained until they are removed from the United States according to the Act, or until they are determined no longer to pose a threat to national security. This measure, which is the equivalent of denying bail to violent offenders, will prevent dangerous aliens from being able to mingle among the American citizens that they would harm.

Finally, I am today asking the Secretary of State to designate 46 groups as terrorist organizations under the USA Patriot Act. All these groups have committed or planned violent terrorist acts, or serve as fronts for terrorist organizations.

The groups to be designated as terrorist organizations include those linked to the al Qaeda network, whose assets the President has frozen, pursuant to an executive order. The remainder of the groups to be designated have been found by the Department of State, in its "Patterns of Global Terrorism" report to have engaged—to have been engaged in terrorist activity. Designating these groups as terrorist organizations will enable us to prevent aliens who are affiliated with them from entering the United States.

In addition, any aliens who are inadmissible because of their affiliation with these groups at the time they manage to enter our country would also be subject to removal. These restrictions apply to groups' representatives and members. Also inadmissible are aliens who use their positions of prominence to endorse terrorist activities.[4]

Other provisions of the act reduced or eliminated restrictions on law enforcement agencies to conduct searches of emails, telephone conversations, and medical, financial, and other records. It also eased restrictions on foreign intelligence gathering in the United States and expanded the Secretary of the Treasury's authority to regulate financial transactions of domestic and foreign individuals, groups, and governments.

Two years after the passage of the Patriot Act, the Justice Department contemplated asking Congress for sweeping new powers for the federal government in conducting investigations and surveillance inside the United States. Titled the Domestic Security Enhancement Act, it quickly became known as the Patriot Act II.[5]

In an opinion piece in *New York Magazine* dated February 23, 2003, one writer stated, "An American citizen suspected of being a part of a terrorist conspiracy could be held by investigators without anyone being notified. He could simply disappear."[6]

The ACLU and other organizations issued an overview of the proposed law as they saw it.[7]

> The government would no longer be required to disclose the identity of anyone, even an American citizen detained in connection with a terror investigation, until criminal charges are filed, no matter how long it takes (sec 201).
>
> Current court limits on local police spying on religious and political activity would be repealed (sec. 312).
>
> The government would be allowed to obtain credit records and library records without a warrant (sec. 126, 128, 129).
>
> Wiretaps without any court order for up to fifteen days after a terror attack would be permissible (sec. 103).
>
> Release of information about health/safety hazards posed by chemical and other plants would be restricted (sec. 202).
>
> The reach of an already overbroad definition of terrorism would be expanded—individuals engaged in civil disobedience could risk losing their citizenship (sec. 501); their organization could be subject to wiretapping (sec. 120, 121) and asset seizure (sec. 428).
>
> Americans could be extradited, searched, and wiretapped at the behest of foreign nations, whether or not treaties allow it (sec. 321, 322).
>
> Lawful immigrants would be stripped of the right to a fair deportation hearing and federal courts would not be allowed to

review immigration rulings (sec. 503, 504).

The Patriot Act II never became law and many of the provisions of the original act expired in 2005. Congress reauthorized most of the provisions of the Patriot Act when it passed the USA Patriot and Terrorism Prevention Reauthorization Act of 2005.[8] The second reauthorization act, The USA Patriot Act Additional Reauthorizing Amendments Act of 2006,[9] amended the first reauthorization and was passed in February 2006.

Once the Patriot Act was signed into law, it became the target of hundreds of lawsuits. Over 150 communities, including several major cities and three states passed resolutions denouncing the Patriot Act as an assault on civil liberties. The ACLU has filed dozens of lawsuits, including one that asks the courts to invalidate provisions of the act that threaten privacy or due process.

The Humanitarian Law Project[10] filed a lawsuit on behalf of human rights activists who were working with members of groups the Justice Department had designated as terror groups. In a 6–3 decision, the Supreme Court upheld the constitutionality of that part of the Patriot Act which outlaws the provision of material support to designated terrorist organizations, stating it does not violate free speech and free association protections of the First Amendment, and is not unconstitutionally vague. The majority opinion written by Chief Justice Roberts says that Congress intentionally wrote the statute with a broad sweep to outlaw material support to terror groups in any form, including assistance or expertise that might help nudge the group toward nonviolence.[11]

Justice Roberts quoted a congressional finding that supported his broad interpretation of the statute. "Foreign organizations that engage in terrorist activity are so tainted by their criminal conduct that any contribution to such an organization facilitates that conduct."[12]

Judge Breyer dissented stating, "The majority's broad reading of the statute raises grave doubt about its constitutionality. I would read the statute as criminalizing First Amendment protected pure speech and association only when the defendant knows or intends that those activities will assist the organization's unlawful terrorist activities."[13]

Another controversial aspect of the USA Patriot Act is the immigration provision that allows for the indefinite detention of any alien who the Attorney General believes may cause a terrorist act. Though the rationale for arresting and detaining aliens during the war years may be different than the post 9/11 era, the results are the same. Innocent people are arrested and deprived of the freedoms and rights guaranteed by the U.S. Constitution.

The full effect of the Patriot Act on the civil liberties of Americans and others living in the United States is unknown. Like the Espionage Act of 1917, the Sedition Act of 1918, the Smith Act, and the executive orders put into place by President Roosevelt, the Patriot Act opens the door for the government to abuse its power and violate those civil liberties guaranteed by the Constitution.

The war in Europe ended in May 1945, and Harry S. Truman had replaced Roosevelt as President of the United States. It was then up to him to decide what to do with the German Americans still held in the internment camps. Never one to mince words, Truman announced that, "The United States has no use for untrustworthy residents. If they were bad news before, they are still bad news now."[14]

Even though the war was over and the German aliens no longer posed a threat to the security of the United States, on July 14, 1945, Truman issued Presidential Proclamation 2655[15] stating that "all alien enemies within the limits of the United States who shall be deemed dangerous to the public peace and safety, may be required to depart therefrom." This proclamation gave the government the authority to repatriate any enemy alien it considered a dangerous enemy during the war.

During the Latin American Conference on Problems of War and Peace, Truman included the kidnapped enemy aliens from Latin America to be repatriated. On September 8, 1945, he issued Presidential Proclamation 2662.[16] The proclamation stated:

> All alien enemies now within the continental limits of the United States who were sent here from other American Republics for restraint and repatriation pursuant to international commitments of the United States Government and for the security of the United States, and its associated powers and who are within the territory of the United States without admission under the

immigration laws are, if their continued residence in the Western Hemisphere is deemed by the Secretary of State to be prejudicial to the future security or welfare of the Americas, as prescribed in Resolution VII of the Inter-America Conference on Problems of War and Peace, subject upon the order of the Secretary of State to removal to destinations outside the limits of the Western Hemisphere in territory of the enemy governments to which or to the principles of which they have adhered. The Department of Justice and all other appropriate agencies of the United States Government are directed to render assistance to the Secretary of State in the prompt effectuation of such orders of removal.

This meant that the detainees the U.S. government had kidnapped from Latin America would not be returning to their countries of residence—and in many cases, those countries did not want them back. Eight months later, Proclamation 2662 was superseded by Proclamation 2685.[17]

All alien enemies within the continental limits of the United States brought here from other American republics after December 7, 1941, who are within the territory of the United States without admission under the immigration laws, shall, if their continued residence in the Western Hemisphere is deemed by the Secretary of State to be prejudicial to the future security or welfare of the Americas, be subject upon the order of the Secretary of State to removal from the United States and may be required to depart there from in accordance with such regulations as the Secretary of State may prescribe.

In all cases in which the Secretary of State shall have ordered the removal of an enemy alien under the authority of this proclamation or in which the Attorney General shall have ordered the removal of an enemy alien under the authority of Proclamation 2655 of July 14, 1945, thirty days shall be considered, and is hereby declared to be a reasonable time for such alien enemy to effect the recovery, disposal, and removal of his goods and effects, and for his departure.

This proclamation supersedes Proclamation No. 2662 of September 8, 1945, entitled "Removal of Alien Enemies."

Truman took the enemy alien issue out of the hands of the Justice Department and turned it over to the State Department with orders to conduct hearings to determine who should be repatriated to Germany and who should remain in America. Those internees determined to be too dangerous to remain in the United States were notified that they would be deported and were given a printed notice that stated:

> Based upon the evidence considered at your earlier alien enemy hearing or hearings, it has been determined that you should be removed and repatriated to the country of your nationality.
>
> Prior to the issuance of a final order for your removal and repatriation, you are entitled to a hearing before a hearing board appointed by the Attorney General . . . to present evidence to show that you are not dangerous to the public peace and safety of the United States.[18]

The acknowledgment form attached to the removal notice stated that the recipient had received the notice of determination of removal from the United States and repatriation to the country of their nationality.[19] It also contained a request for a repatriation hearing at which the accused could present evidence for staying the final order for repatriation.

Many of the internees decided to fight the removal order. They had no desire to return to a country in ruins that many of them had never seen. Food and clothing were in short supply and with limited housing available, Germany was a miserable place to spend the bitter winters of 1945 and 1946. Since the Germans didn't trust them, the internees were greeted with suspicion and hostility.

A small group of twenty-four internees from Crystal City organized a committee to fight the deportation order. Along with internees from other camps, they pooled their resources and hired James L. Laughlin, a lawyer from the Citizens' Protective League (CPL) to challenge the constitutionality of the deportation program. Laughlin met with Attorney General Tom Clark and requested that all internees be released on parole, but Clark denied the request. Laughlin asked for individual cases to be reviewed by the courts. Clark denied that request too.

The CPL took the case before the U.S. Court of Appeals, but the court ruled against them. In the case of Citizens' Protective League et al. v. Tom Clark, Attorney General of the United States,[20] the court ruled that the internees were considered dangerous to the public, now and in the future. The ruling opened the door for the authorities at Crystal City to serve all outstanding removal orders on the Germans, but not the Japanese or those cases stayed by court action. All internees the government considered dangerous were declared deportees and were told that they could never return to the United States except to visit. However, any internee who volunteered to be exchanged would be allowed to return someday.

Hundreds of internees scheduled for deportation continued to fight the removal order. Some argued that their deportation was illegal because they were denied lawyers and the right to cross-examine government witnesses. Federal courts and the U.S. Court of Appeals ruled against them. A few internees filed a writ of habeas corpus claiming the government did not have a legal right to deport them because their native countries were no longer enemy countries. The internees lost on that one too when the courts ruled that Latin American internees were alien enemies who could be detained and deported.

Thanks to the courts, the government then had carte blanche to deport the internees against their will. Thus, 897 Germans, 513 Japanese, and 37 Italians were given informal hearings and shipped, not to their homes in Latin America, but to the former Axis nations. Most were outraged and angered at this travesty of justice. Kidnapped from their homes, brought to the United States, and detained in prison camps for years, they were then summarily shipped to war-ravaged countries many of them had never seen.

The first groups of internees to be repatriated were volunteers. They were transferred from Crystal City, Texas to Ellis Island on November 7, 1945. The second group did not volunteer, nor did they go willingly. As the deportations continued and the internees were paroled, released, or repatriated, the Immigration and Naturalization Service began to shut down the camps. Those internees still held by the INS were transferred to camps that remained open and then to Ellis Island to await a decision on their cases. The last German Americans were not released from Ellis Island until July 1948, three years after hostilities with Germany ceased.

The release of the last internee from Ellis Island should have been the end of the story. Unfortunately, McCarthyism reared its ugly head when Senator Joseph McCarthy took up where previous administrations and congressional committees left off. McCarthyism was a term that described the political action of making accusations of disloyalty, subversion, or treason without proper regard for evidence. Originally coined to criticize the anti-communist hearings of Senator McCarthy, the term is now used to describe reckless, unsubstantiated accusations and demagogic attacks on the character and patriotism of political opponents.

During the McCarthy era, thousands of Americans were accused of being communists or communist sympathizers. They were aggressively investigated and questioned before dozens of government committees and agencies. The primary targets were government employees, the entertainment industry, educators, and union activists. Suspicions were given credibility despite inconclusive or questionable evidence, including witnesses who lied under oath. Many of the victims of the senator's committee suffered the loss of employment; destruction of careers; and, in some cases, imprisonment. The courts later overturned most of the guilty verdicts after certain laws were declared unconstitutional, or when it was determined the verdict was made for reasons that were later declared illegal or actionable, or when extra-legal procedures were called into disrepute.

The House Committee on Un-American Activities (HUAC) was the most prominent and active committee investigating anti-communist activities, and its investigations overshadowed the activities of the McCarthy committees. The tactics of the HUAC resembled those used by the Justice Department in its treatment of alien enemies in the 1940s.

HUAC attained its greatest notoriety with an investigation into the film industry. In October 1947, the committee subpoenaed screenwriters, directors, and other movie industry professionals to testify about their membership in the Communist Party and to name names of others who belonged to the party. As witnesses were called to testify, they were each asked if they had ever been a member of the Communist Party.

The first ten witnesses called to testify decided not to cooperate with the committee. These men, who became known as the "Hollywood Ten" cited the First Amendment guarantee of free speech, which they believed protected them from being required to answer the committee's questions. The committee responded by citing them for contempt of Congress. Two of the witnesses were sentenced to six months in jail and the remaining eight to one year. Witnesses who were determined not to cooperate with the committee claimed the protection of the Fifth Amendment against self-incrimination. It protected them against contempt of Congress citation, but was considered grounds for dismissal from their jobs by government agencies and private employers.

There is no way to estimate the number of victims of McCarthyism or the HUAC. Hundreds were imprisoned and ten or twelve thousand lost their jobs. Simply being subpoenaed to appear before the HUAC or one of the other committees was sufficient cause to be fired. Many of the individuals who went to jail, lost their jobs, or appeared before the committees did have connections of some kind with the Communist Party, but like the alien enemies of World Wars I and II, the vast majority of them were innocent.

During the late 1960s and early 1970s, America was embroiled in a national debate over excessive government surveillance of its citizens. Concerned with these excesses, the U.S. Senate established an eleven-member panel known as the Church Committee[21] to investigate government surveillance programs. Named for Senator Frank Church, the committee uncovered numerous unconstitutional spying activities such as the National Security Agency sting known as *Operation Shamrock*.[22]

Operation Shamrock was a covert, domestic intelligence gathering operation that monitored all telegraphic data entering or exiting the United States. The program was created as a military intelligence operation during World War II. In the months before war in Europe broke out, the Armed Forces Security Agency requested permission from ITT World Communications, Western Union International, and RCA Global to tap their international cables to eavesdrop on foreign coded transmissions. As the war progressed, intelligence agents intercepted all civilian and military wire traffic.

President Truman created the National Security Agency (NSA)

in 1952, which immediately took control of the program. If the NSA found messages that were of interest to other agencies, that information was disseminated to the FBI, CIA, Secret Service, Bureau of Narcotics and Dangerous Drugs, and Department of Defense. NSA personnel intercepted and analyzed approximately 150,000 messages per month. This practice was continued until May 1975 when it was exposed by the Church Committee and terminated by Lew Allen, the director of the NSA. It is important to note that the courts did not authorize the wiretaps and no warrants were ever issued.

Following in the footsteps of his predecessors, President Gerald Ford secretly authorized the FBI to conduct warrantless domestic wiretaps for foreign intelligence and counter intelligence. In a recently declassified "Top Secret, Eyes Only"[23] memorandum, dated December 19, 1974, Ford authorized Attorney General William Saxbe "to approve, without prior judicial warrants, specific electronic surveillance within the United States which may be requested by the Director of the Federal Bureau of Investigation." In the memo to Saxbe, Ford wrote, "I have been advised by you (Saxbe) and by the Department of State that such surveillance is consistent with the Constitution and the laws and treaties of the United States."

The purpose of this warrantless wiretap was to give the Justice Department and the FBI the power to spy on Americans or foreigners in the United States who were spying for foreign countries or political groups. Electronic surveillance in the United States could only be authorized by the personal approval of the Attorney General upon submission of a written request by the Director of the FBI, stating complete justification for the surveillance, identification of the agency requesting the action, and the presidential appointee initiating the request. Authorization would be granted once the Attorney General was satisfied that the following criteria had been met.[24]

A. That the requested electronic surveillance is necessary
   To protect the nation against actual or potential attack or other hostile acts of a foreign power.
   To obtain foreign intelligence information deemed essential to the security of the nation.
   To protect national security information against foreign intelligence activities.

> To obtain information which the Secretary of State (or a presidential appointee who is his personally designated representative) or the Assistant to the President for National Security Affairs has certified is necessary for the conduct of foreign affairs matters which are important to the national security of the United States.
>
> B. That the subject of the electronic surveillance is assisting a foreign power or foreign-based political group, or plans unlawful activity directed against a foreign power or foreign-based political group.
>
> C. That the minimum physical intrusion necessary to obtain the information sought will be used.

John Laprise, a visiting assistant professor in the communications department at Northwestern University, uncovered the memo in the National Archives. He said in an interview that, "the document brings to light previously unknown information about the Ford administration's policy on warrantless wiretaps. Ford was completely motivated by defending against the Cold War threat of the Soviet Union. This could be Bush after 9/11 or Obama after becoming president . . . but it's President Ford thirty-five years ago, coping with Cold War struggles. It's really a stunning document that raises all sorts of questions."[25]

In what appears to be a turnaround in his attitude toward warrantless wiretapping and surveillance, Ford supported the passage of the Foreign Intelligence Surveillance Act of 1978 (FISA).[26] This act placed restrictions on wiretapping and required law enforcement to obtain permission from a special court to conduct domestic intelligence surveillance.

Signed into law by President Carter in 1978, the act was created as a direct result of Senate committee investigations into the legality of domestic intelligence activities. It was also in response to President Nixon's violation of the Fourth Amendment to the Constitution when he used federal resources to spy on his political enemies, activists, and anti-war groups.

The act provided for judicial and congressional oversight of the government's covert surveillance activities of foreign entities and individuals in the United States, while still maintaining the secrecy necessary to protect national security. It allowed surveillance within the United States for up to one year without a court order unless the surveillance would acquire the contents of any communication to which a United States citizen was a party. If a U.S. citizen was involved, judicial authorization was required within seventy-two hours after surveillance was requested.

What made this act different from previously passed legislation was the creation of the Foreign Intelligence Surveillance Court (FISC).[27] It was the job of this court to oversee requests for surveillance warrants by federal police agencies (primarily the FBI) against suspected foreign intelligence agents inside the United States.

Located within the offices of the Department of Justice, the FISC is currently staffed by eleven judges appointed seven-year terms by the Chief Justice of the Supreme Court. Proceedings before the FISC are *ex parte* and non-adversarial. The court hears evidence presented by the Department of Justice and neither the records of information collected nor the results of the hearings are ever released to the public.

Since the passage of FISA in 1978, a number of new wiretap and surveillance acts are under consideration or have been signed into law. Three new bills have been introduced in Congress in an attempt to ease the possibility of abuse by government officials and to clarify the language of earlier bills. The Terrorist Surveillance Act of 2006 gives the president additional limited statutory authority to conduct electronic surveillance on suspected terrorists in the United States subject to enhanced Congressional oversight. The National Security Surveillance Act of 2006 amends FISA to grant retroactive amnesty for warrantless surveillance conducted under presidential authority and provides court (FISC) jurisdiction to review, authorize, and oversee electronic surveillance programs. The Foreign Intelligence Surveillance Improvement and Enhancement Act of 2006 asserts that FISA is the exclusive authority to conduct foreign intelligence surveillance.

Many of the tactics employed by the government in the name of national security in 1915 are still in play today. The Espionage Act of 1917 and the Sedition Act of 1918 formed the foundation for the Patriot Act, the Foreign Intelligence Surveillance Act, and similar legislation. This legislation of fear and suspicion resulting from two world wars, the Red Scare, and the War on Terror continue to impact the lives of American citizens far into the 21st century.

Weary from the horrors of the First World War, America isolated itself from the rest of the world in the 1920s and passed laws to keep those considered to be undesirable elements out of the country. Congress developed stringent measures to deny legal entry to Mexican laborers. The Immigration Act of 1924 barred foreigners who were ineligible for American citizenship from entering the United States. This provision of the law effectively ended the immigration of all Asians and inflamed the passions of the anti-Japanese press. Other provisions of the law drastically reduced the allowable quota for immigrants from Southern and Eastern Europe while welcoming newcomers from Britain, Ireland, and Northern Europe.

Perceived failure of the federal government to enforce current immigration policy and secure the borders has become a political hot potato. There is some concern that the paranoia and racial and ethnic hatred that fueled the immigration issues of the 1920s could be revived to influence a backlash against illegal immigrants in America today. Because the individual states believe the federal government is not enforcing current immigration law, they are now taking action to pass and enforce their own immigration laws. Until the Congress of the United States addresses this issue and passes comprehensive immigration reform, it will be up to the courts to intervene in the battle between the federal government and the individual states.

The laws governing every aspect of American life and the freedoms that Americans cherish are defined by amendments to the Constitution. Every president from Woodrow Wilson to the present occupant of the White House has violated one or more provisions of the Constitution in the name of national security at one time or another during their time in office.

During World War I, the First Amendment came under attack when American citizens were arrested and jailed for speaking out against the Wilson Administration and America's involvement in the war. President Roosevelt denied due process when he ordered the arrest and internment of thousands of innocent aliens and American citizens in prison camps. After the attack on Pearl Harbor, Roosevelt together with the U.S. Army declared martial law, suspended the writ of habeas corpus and the right of free speech, and arrested and interned hundreds of innocent German and Japanese residents, many of them American citizens.

The America of the 21st century bears little resemblance to the America of 1916, but with regard to government actions against its own citizens, not much has changed. Aided and abetted by the courts, the government can and often does act with impunity. If history has taught us anything, it is that the government will continue to violate the Constitution whenever it deems the best interests of the American people to be at stake—rightfully or wrongly.

The wars in Iraq and Afghanistan, illegal immigration, the dismal economy, failed government policies, and a government that seems indifferent to its citizens are all driving the anger of the American people. The principles that America was built on and the Constitution that guarantees the freedoms that so many Americans fought and died for appear to have been ignored or forgotten.

The events of the last 100 years are a matter of record. The abuse of power by our government and the attacks on our civil liberties are well documented. In the name of national security, our elected officials have suspended those freedoms guaranteed to us in the Constitution, often with the consent of the American people. We should learn the lessons of history and heed the words of Ben Franklin. "Any society that would give up an essential liberty for temporary security deserves neither liberty nor security."

NOTES

1. Eberhard Fuhr, *My Internment by the U.S. Government*, 2008.
2. Espionage Act, USC 18, PL 1, CH 37, Stat. 217, June 15, 1917, Sedition Act, Vol. XL, pp 553 ff, May 16, 1918.
3. USA Patriot Act (USAPA) P.L. 107-56 H.R. 3162, October 25, 2001.
4. John Ashcroft, U.S. Attorney General, Powers of Patriot Act I, Formation of Foreign Terrorist Tracking Task Force, Department of Justice, October 31, 2001.

5. Domestic Security Enhancement Act, January 2003.
6. Mathew Brzezinski, Fortress America, *New York Times Magazine,* February 23, 2003.
7. ACLU Patriot Act Fact Sheet, March 28, 2003.
8. USA Patriot Improvement and Reauthorization Act of 2005, HR 3199, P.L. 109-177, March 9, 2006.
9. USA Patriot Act Additional Reauthorizing Amendments Act of 2005, S. 2271, P.L. 109-178, March 9, 2006.
10. Holder vs. Humanitarian Law Project, U.S. Supreme Court 05-56753, June 4, 2009.
11. "Supreme Court Upholds Controversial Part of Patriot Act," www.sodahead.com/Supreme Court.
12. Ibid.
13. Ibid.
14. Statement by President Harry S. Truman prior to signing proclamation 2655, July 14, 1945.
15. Harry S. Truman, Presidential Proclamation 2655, Removal of Enemy Aliens, Section 21, Title 50, USC, July 14, 1945.
16. Harry S. Truman, Presidential Proclamation 2662, Removal of Enemy Aliens, Section 4067 of Revised Statutes of the United States. Section 21, Title 50 USC, September 8, 1945, (superseded by Proclamation 2685).
17. Harry s. Truman, Presidential Proclamation 2685, Removal of Enemy Aliens, 11 FR., 4079, 3 CFR, 1943–1948, Comp., April 11, 1946.
18. Department of Justice, War Division, Notice of Repatriation of Alien Enemy, Acknowledgement of Notice and Request for Alien Enemy repatriation Hearing.
19. Ibid.
20. Citizens Protective League et al vs. Tom Clark, Attorney general of the United States, 5 Mass. App. Ct. 43, January 31, 1977.
21. Operation Shamrock, Encyclopedia of Espionage, Intelligence, and Security, www.espionageinfo.com/Nt-Pa//operation shamrock.
22. Ibid.
23. Ford Memo, for the Attorney General, The White House, Washington, DC, December 19, 1974.
24. Ibid.
25. Jerry Ford Okays Warrantless Wire Taps in U.S. www.politicsdaily.com/2010/04/03/president-ford.
26. Foreign Intelligence Service Act of 1978, (FISA) P.L. 95-511, 92 Stat. 1783, October 25, 1978.
27. Ibid.

List of Internment Camps/Detention Centers

State	Camp	Organization
California	Angel Island	Military
	San Pedro	INS
	San Isidro	INS
	Sharp Park	INS
	Tujunga (Tuna Canyon)	INS
Colorado	Denver	INS
	Fort Logan	Military
Connecticut	Hartford Community Center	INS
Cuba	Pine Island	INS
Florida	Fort Barrancas	Military
	Miami	INS
	Tampa	INS
Georgia	Fort Oglethorpe	Military
	Fort Screven	Military
Hawaii	Honolulu	Military
	Sand Island	Military
Illinois	Chicago	INS
Louisiana	Algiers	INS/State Department
	New Orleans	INS/State Department
Massachusetts	East Boston	INS
Maryland	Fort Howard	Military
	Fort Meade	Military
Mexico	Nuevo Laredo	INS/State Department
Michigan	Detroit	INS
Minnesota	St. Paul County Jail	INS
Missouri	Kansas City	INS
	St. Louis County Jail	INS
Montana	Fort Missoula	Military
Nebraska	Fort Cook	Military
	Omaha	INS
New Jersey	Gloucester City	INS
New Mexico	Fort Stanton	Military
	Lordsburg	Military

New York	Buffalo	INS
	Camp Upton	Military
	Ellis Island	INS
	Niagara Falls	INS
	Syracuse	INS
North Carolina	Asheville	INS
North Dakota	Fort Lincoln	Military
Ohio	Cincinnati	INS
	Cleveland	INS
Oklahoma	Fort Sill	Military
	McAlester	Military
	Stringtown	Military
Oregon	Portland	INS
Pennsylvania	Nanticoke	INS
	Philadelphia	INS
	Pittsburgh	INS
Puerto Rico	San Juan	Military
Tennessee	Camp Forrest	Military
Texas	Crystal City	INS
	Fort Bliss	Military
	Fort Sam, Houston	Military
	Houston	INS
	Kennedy	INS
	Laredo	INS
	San Antonio	INS
	Seagoville	INS
Utah	Salt Lake City	INS
Washington	Seattle	INS
	Spokane	INS
	Sullivan Lake	Military
West Virginia	White Sulphur Springs	INS/State Department
Wisconsin	Camp McCoy	Military
	Milwaukee	INS

This list was compiled by Arthur D. Jacobs, author of *The Prison Called Hohenasperg*, 2005; updated 2007.

BIBLIOGRAPHY

BOOKS

Christgau, John. *Enemies—World War II Alien Internment.* Iowa State University Press, 1955.

Donald, Heidi Gurcke. *We Were Not the Enemy: Remembering the United States' Latin American Civilian Internment Program of World War II.* iUniverse.com., 2006.

Fox, Stephen. *Uncivil Liberties: Italian Americans Under Siege During World War II.* Universal Publishers, USA, 2000.

Friedman, Max Paul. *Nazis and Good Neighbors: The U.S. Campaign against Germans in Latin America during World War II.* Cambridge University Press, 2003.

Gardiner, C. Harvey. *Pawns in a Triangle of Hate.* Seattle: University of Washington Press, 1981.

Jacobs, Arthur D. *The Prison Called Hohenasperg: An American Boy Betrayed by His Government during World War II.* Universal Publishers, USA, 1999.

Kramer, Arnold. *Undue Process: The Untold Story of America's German Alien Internees.* New York: Rowman & Littlefield, 1997.

Schmitz, John Eric. *The Enemy Among Us: The Relocation and Repatriation of German, Italian, and Japanese Americans During the Second world War.* The American University, 2007.

NEWSPAPERS

"Nations to Meet in Rio." *Salinas Index Journal,* January 2, 1942.

"Photo and Alien Card Necessary." *Salinas Index Journal*, January 20, 1942.

"Governor in Action to Curb California Aliens." *Salinas Index Journal*, January 30, 1942.

"69 More Areas in California Closed by Law." *Salinas Index Journal*, January 31, 1942.

"West Begins Evacuation of Enemy Aliens." *Salinas Index Journal*, February 9, 1942.

"FBI Rounds Up Aliens: Fishermen Taken From L.A. Port." *Salinas Index Journal*, February 2, 1942.

"Alien Identification Work Speeded." *Salinas Index Journal*, February 5, 1942.

"Regulations Listed for Enemy Aliens, Photograph Will Go on Certificate." *Salinas Index Journal*, February 5, 1942.

"138 Officers Hunt Contraband in Valley Round Up." *Salinas Index Journal*, February 9, 1942.

"Orders Go into Effect on February 15." *Salinas Index Journal*, February 11, 1942.

"Evacuation of 10,000 Enemy Aliens to Begin." *Salinas Index Journal*, February 23, 1942.

"Brazilians Raid Stores of Germans." *Salinas Index Journal*, March 12, 1942.

"4163 Enemy Aliens Held." *New York Times*, March 19, 1943.

"FBI Round Up Nets 31 German Aliens." *New York Times*, June 6, 1943.

"Nazi Family of Five Seized in Brooklyn." New *York Times*, June 27, 1943.

"FBI Seizes New York Pair." *New York Times*, September 21, 1943.

"Thirteen Germans Seized in New Jersey." *New York Times*, November 19, 1943.

"FBI Seizes Germans as Dangerous Aliens." *New York Times*, December 2, 1943.

"FBI Reports Seizure of Twenty-four Alleged Nazis: Woman with Medal from Hitler Included." *New York Times*, September 28, 1944.

"Thirty-nine German Aliens Sentenced." *New York Times*, December 6, 1944.

"Deportees, POWs Head for Germany." *New York Times*, September 16, 1945.

ABOUT THE AUTHOR

A native of Wildwood, New Jersey, Russell served in the United States Air Force during the early years of the Cold War. He was actively involved in the Apollo moon landings and the space shuttle program. He served as a technical advisor to the German Air Force and during the height of the Cold War was assigned to remote locations to gather intelligence data on Soviet submarines and nuclear underwater tests for the CIA and other government agencies.

Russell graduated from New Mexico State University with a degree in management and teaches a class in creative writing at Dixie State College in St. George, Utah. He is married and makes his home among the magnificent red mountains of Southern Utah.